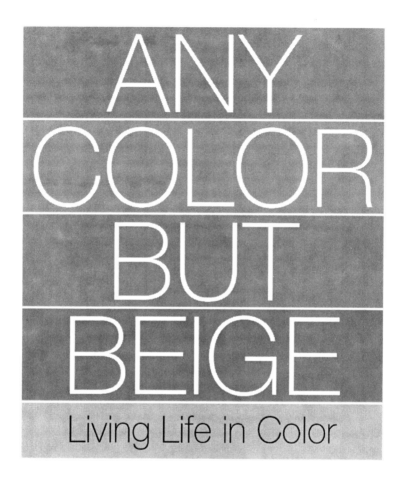

ANY COLOR BUT BEIGE

Living Life in Color

By Catherine Larose

First Edition – July 2011

ISBN

978-1-77067-488-2 (Hardcover)

978-1-77067-489-9 (Paperback)

978-1-77067-490-5 (eBook)

This book is a femoir, and in some places, to keep the story moving forward, I've taken a few liberties. In some cases, I have altered characters, places and professions. In other cases, I have combined characters and events, or presented some events out of sequence to protect the identities of certain individuals. A few events are creative recreation, and are not intended to portray actual events or people but serve as necessary transitions for the story. Dialogue has been recreated from memory and, in some cases, has been compressed to convey the substance of what was said or what occurred.

Library and Archives Canada Cataloguing in Publication

Larose, Catherine

Any Color But Beige: Living Life in Color

ISBN 978-1-77067-490-5

1. Larose, Catherine. 2. Divorced women—Biography. 3. Dating (Social customs). I. Title.

HQ811.5.L37A3 2011a 306.89'3092 C2011-903754-8

Café Girl Books

www.cafegirlchronicles.wordpress.com

Edited by Melva McLean, Proofread by Lana Okerlund, Cover Design by Steven Schultz,
Cover Illustration by Helen Samson, Use of Red-Soled Shoes on Cover Courtesy of M. Christian Louboutin

Published by:
FriesenPress

Suite 300 – 852 Fort Street

Victoria, BC, Canada V8W 1H8

www.friesenpress.com

Distributed to the trade by The Ingram Book Company

for my grandmother
Vincenza C. Ricci

TABLE OF CONTENTS

INTRODUCTION

I've always wanted to be an artist but I learned early on that I have no talent for drawing or painting. Undeterred by my lack of natural talent I read several "how-to" books on the subject. I learned that it wasn't so much my inability to put pencil or brush to paper that held me back; it was my limited ability *to see*. Artists *see* the lines and edges, the light and shadows, the play of color in life. They use a variety of materials to express what they see.

In an effort to express my own vision, I decided to become a writer instead, which in some ways amounts to the same thing. My chosen medium is words. It wasn't until recently, however, that it occurred to me that my worldview was perhaps myopic and limited to an off-white and neutral palette. I was looking at life but not really seeing it. Like most people, I lived a mostly beige existence.

Occasionally I'd add a dash of color like red when I was feeling brave, green when I envied others' happiness, or blue when I thought mine was not the life I was supposed to have. I had the nagging feeling that a fuller, richer and more colorful life was out there waiting for me if only I had the courage to choose it. If only it were that simple.

With every passing day I could feel it slipping further away from me. Every time I looked at the second hand on my watch, I saw it sweeping around the numbers at warp speed. Wait! Wait! I silently screamed. Yet I did nothing. Another day gone; another opportunity lost.

For many years I held various positions as a writer in advertising, public relations and marketing, for some big companies too. It sounds glamorous, but life in corporate North America can be bland because companies and people are naturally risk averse. That used to be me. Tired of hitting dead ends in the corporate cubicle maze, I took a chance and moved over to sales.

Now I sell color. I sell color to paint companies in the form of paint chips—those little color swatches found in home improvement centers, hardware stores and retail shops.

"Wow," someone will say. "I never thought of that but I guess someone has to do it."

That someone is me. I know a lot about color: its history, its meaning, how it affects people, how a certain color becomes a trend. I speak the language of color to customers in Europe, Asia, Africa, the Americas and Australia.

Professionally my life has been full of color—colorful places, people and experiences—but personally I was with a partner who was basically color blind—the blind leading the blind, so to speak. No matter what I did to add a little color to our lives I was always met with polite resistance. Who could argue with a man who said no so nicely? I never could.

For years I carried on out of habit, fear and guilt. I spent most of my time pursuing a colorful life on the road in an effort to avoid the dreariness of my everyday existence at home. A few years ago, on a business trip to Paris, I had an epiphany as I watched the sun set. Its pastel hues washed the sky like watercolors on a canvas. I wanted to fold it up, put it in my pocket and take it with me as a reminder of what could be.

In a moment of clarity—the kind that allows one a brief glimpse of the future—I saw one long, lonely stretch of desert highway that was a sepia-toned snapshot of my life. Is this what you want for the next 20 years? I asked myself. You're only in your mid-40s; 20 years is another lifetime.

That was the day I decided it was time to live my life in color, to use every crayon in the box, to go outside the lines, and to begin by painting the bedroom a magnificent Bordeaux red, a color as complex as the wine itself. I knew my husband preferred white walls, but this time I wouldn't take a polite no for an answer.

This "femoir," as I call it, is based on real events in my life. The story is divided into four distinct parts and unfolds chronologically. Each part is named after a point in time on my own life spectrum. Colorful destination anecdotes introduce each part and establish the theme for what follows. They also allow me to explain what it means to sell color.

In some cases I've taken a few liberties to advance the story. In others, I've changed or combined characters or altered professions, places and events. In spite of these changes you can be sure that, since my divorce, I have lived a colorful life.

—Cat Larose, Montreal, January 2011

DESTINATION: PARIS

The skyline was festooned with ribbons of pink, peach and mauve light. I was sitting in a corner office on the 14th floor of one of the ubiquitous office towers in La Défense, a major business district of Paris. As I stared out at the famous Grande Arche de la Défense, I felt like I could disintegrate into a thousand particles of happiness. I was working in Paris. Mind you, it was only a business trip and I was due to return home to Cleveland the next day, but I was there nonetheless.

Earlier I had delivered a color trend presentation to a skeptical audience from a high-end furniture design company, and I'd done it *en français*. Giving a presentation in English is tough enough; doing it in another language doubles the fear factor. The marketing team had arrived with their minds made up: there was nothing new I could tell them. Or so they'd thought.

I'd said the same silent prayer I always say before every presentation: "Dear God, please don't let me sound stupid." (No matter how many times I make presentations I still get stage fright.) I took a deep breath, smiled with more confidence than I felt and started.

I had talked about color intuition—an idea that went against the popular theory of trend forecasts that identify one or two things in the marketplace driving color choices in the home furnishings industry. That was old preaching. I'd come to proclaim the gospel of individuation—your color, your choice.

"People gravitate toward colors that they like intuitively, that make them feel comfortable, that make them feel at ease," I'd told the group. "Just because the magazines and the market say aqua or lime is the new *in* color doesn't mean you'll buy furniture, paint or appliances in that shade. I bet if I looked at the clothing in your closets I would find the same colors in your houses.

"In fact"—and here I'd pointed at the people seated around the conference table—"I would venture to say that the colors you're wearing right now can be found in the most comfortable rooms of your house."

They'd all looked down at what they were wearing and looked back up at me, reluctantly nodding their heads in agreement.

"This is why the ability to help your customer choose a few colors she is comfortable with is more important than getting her to pick from a large selection of colors that means nothing to her. *N'est-ce pas*?"

The presentation had drawn a polite round of applause. As is customary, I'd thanked everyone for their participation and shook hands in farewell before making my exit to the marketing director's office, where I'd collapsed in his chair, adrenaline still pulsing through my veins.

Once my heartbeat and breathing had returned to normal, I'd distracted myself by swiveling from side to side in the big leather chair while I waited for Le Chef de marketing, Christian Castin, to return. Christian is from the Alsace region of France and thus looks more German than French; the tweed jacket and pipe he sported that day made him look much older than his 35 years.

"Bravo, Cat. Everyone enjoyed your presentation," he'd said as he entered the room.

"Really?"

"Really. Give me about 30 minutes and I'll be back. In the meantime, make yourself, how do you say it, at home? Call back to your office, send e-mails—here's *le mot de passe*," he said as he handed me a slip of paper. "*Voilà*."

"Are we still going to dinner?"

"*Mais oui*. We'll go for drinks first. I have dinner reservations at eight o'clock at Le Chien Qui Fume."

"Only in France would they name a restaurant after a smoking dog."

"But of course." Christian had said as he exited his office.

I twirled around once in the chair behind the oversized glass and chrome desk, stopping in front of the floor-to-ceiling windows. It was dusk, my favorite time of day, and lights were starting to come on in the neighboring office buildings. They gave the entire district an eerie blue glow. I began to imagine what it would be like to live in Paris, to live a different life, to live on my own.

Then reality quickly set in; I had to go home. I unconsciously tensed my shoulders at the thought and my temples started to throb. What's wrong with me? I wondered. I had just finished a three-week road trip to several European and Scandinavian cities. I should have been happy to get home and back into my normal life.

The truth was that I longed for the comforts of a home, just not my home. It wasn't even "our" home. When I looked back over my 20-year marriage to Gabriel, all I saw was a vast desert. Few memories dotted that landscape. Oh sure, there was the occasional cactus, prickly reminders of the times we tolerated each other enough to go on vacation. But even on vacation we would go our separate ways. In Venice, Gabriel could wait hours for the crowds to clear in the Piazza San Marco in order to take the perfect picture. Too impatient to wait, I would visit the Palace of the Doge or tour the city by gondola alone. Gabriel lived his life through a viewfinder. I lived mine live, taking mental pictures and collecting stories.

It had once been so easy to dismiss nagging doubts about my marriage. I would fill the void with projects like learning Spanish, practicing yoga, doing home renovations, volunteering my time and working more than I should. There was always lots of work to do on nights and weekends, and a lot of it was on the road.

The road always beckoned. The road was freedom, if only temporarily. I packed more than my clothes in my suitcase. There was also guilt and loneliness, my constant travel companions. Over time these feelings became harder to ignore. The little bouts of worry, as I called them, were, in fact, panic attacks in disguise. Denial is only a temporary fix.

Most people who knew me thought I had it all: a charming, handsome husband, a beautiful home, an exciting career, a caring family and true friends. And I did. And if they thought I was happy, it wasn't their fault. I'm a good actress, and after years of hard work I'd painstakingly crafted the perfect facade. I had nearly convinced myself that this was the life I was supposed to have. The realization that I'd painted a picture-perfect life with all the wrong colors now hit me like a brain freeze.

I pulled a piece of watered silk fabric from my laptop case and admired the richness of its deep burgundy color and mottled texture. This color would look great in a bedroom—in my bedroom. I sighed. Gabriel was a beige man. What I needed was a room of my own, damn it. A red one.

Before I could give it any further thought, Christian poked his head through the doorway. "Ready?" he asked.

I swiveled the chair back to face the desk and reality.

"As ready as I'll ever be," I said.

In the parking garage, Christian stopped just before a row of cars. "Can you guess which one?" he asked.

I scrutinized them: a Mercedes, a BMW, an Audi and a Peugeot.

"Hmmm." I pointed to the dark blue BMW.

Christian laughed. "Non."

We walked a little farther down the row. "I know," I said. "It's the Audi."

He shook his head. "See! It's there!" He pointed proudly.

"You've got to be kid—"

I stopped myself and looked at him. I was astonished he could fold his six-foot frame into the little white Smart car tucked into the corner.

"Allons y," he said.

Before long we were entering the teeming traffic circle at the Arc de Triomphe. We buzzed into the 12-lane melee like a bee zipping into a hive. We made the first turn on what felt like two wheels. It was surreal. I thought about the improbability of the situation. I mean... really. There I was, a girl from Cleveland, Ohio, racing around Place de l'Étoile in the city of my dreams.

How in the world, I asked myself, did I ever get here?

Part One:
Primary Colors

CHAPTER 1:
THE RED SUITCASE

All you need is a place to hang your hat. —Grandma Vi

My grandmother Vincenza (Vi) lived with us in a large turn-of-the-century house on Cleveland's lower west side. She lived in our house but we lived in her neighborhood, an Italian enclave of extended families, hardworking immigrants and lots of children. My mixed Italian/Irish heritage made me feel at home with families whose names either began or ended with a vowel. O'Malley or Brizzi, it didn't matter; from a very young age I and my siblings, like many of the immigrants who had passed through our neighborhood, were an adaptable lot. We learned to fit in anywhere.

In our neighborhood were two grocery stores complete with butcher shops, two bakeries, my great-Aunt Justina's dry cleaning and tailoring shop, and, best of all, two candy stores with soda fountains. Nearly every home had a grape arbor in the backyard, and my family spent most summer evenings visiting with neighbors and sharing coffee and conversation under a canopy of grape leaves. The adults drank their evening espresso or perhaps a glass of *vino rosso,* and we kids drank freshly squeezed lemonade. Nothing in that neighborhood came from a can or a bottle.

The adults usually spoke English, but they quickly turned to Italian if good gossip was involved. Most emphatic phrases started with the word "*ma*," which is Italian for *but*. I loved the way each phrase was accompanied by the appropriate gesture, like throwing up one's hands in disbelief, or the praying-hands pose, or the open, right-angled hand wave.

"*Ma,* are you crazy?"

"*Ma,* what was he thinking?"

"*Ma,* whatsamattah for you?"

I always ducked when I heard this last one because it was followed by a quick swat to the head.

After finishing her afternoon shift at the local Union Carbide factory, Grandma Vi would come home, get cleaned up, touch up her red nail polish and walk over to the next street to visit with her sisters, my great aunts. She usually took me with her. We made quite a pair, she and I, strolling arm in arm, slowly making our *passeggiata*. She was a dark-haired beauty with olive skin that would remain wrinkle free all her life. I was her little ghost of a granddaughter with pale skin, red hair and large green eyes. I looked like the poster child for Tourism Ireland. My mother would sometimes lean over to Grandma Vi and whisper, "I know I gave birth to her but sometimes I wonder if there wasn't a mix-up at the hospital."

Louisa Brizzi O'Malley; her teased black hair with blond streaks was held in place by a Jackie O headband. She always sported a pair of bright white Keds tennis shoes and never left the house without her make-up on. She was Connie Francis, Annette Funicello and Elizabeth Taylor all rolled into one energetic package. I used to wonder about a potential mix-up too, but it was plain to see I had my mother's patrician features and my father's ruddy Irish complexion. There was no denying it, or me.

At the age of nine I felt very grown up to be included in Grandma Vi's nightly summer ritual, despite the fact that she often stopped to inspect my face.

"Didn't you take a bath?" she asked on one of these evenings.

I nodded. Yes, I'd taken a bath, but those steamy Ohio summer nights made it impossible to keep cool or clean. The blue sailor top and matching pedal pushers that had looked clean just 20 minutes earlier now hung limply on my small frame.

Grandma Vi took a hanky out of her pocketbook and dabbed at a dirt smudge on my cheek. Then she spritzed me with a bottle of her favorite cologne, Emeraude.

"Gram did you hear?" I asked as she fished around for a comb. "They put a man on the moon today."

"Imagine!" she replied. "That's a long way to travel just to get some pecorino cheese when all you have to do is go to Micelli's." She laughed at her own joke, and then grew serious. "Someday you will be hopping off and on airplanes just like we used to do with the streetcars. You'll see. We're launching you this week. You will have something in common with those astronauts."

That night's visit to Aunt Justina's had a special purpose. We were borrowing a small suitcase because I was about to leave for camp. It was a dream come true. I couldn't wait to be on my own, to leave the confines of our big, old, noisy house filled with kids, adults, dogs and cats. No dusting, no diapers, no folding clothes or picking up someone else's toys. No responsibilities.

I would taste the freedom of a foreign place, at least foreign to me. I would trade in concrete sidewalks and parked cars for the quiet of the countryside one hour's drive from home. There would be trees instead of telephone wires. There would be arts and crafts, hiking and swimming, stars and crickets. I would meet new people. For the first time I would be on my own, without family or friends—except for Donna.

Donna Peterson was one of our few non-Italian neighbors and a protestant. That summer she also happened to be my new best friend because, for some reason now long forgotten, I was on the outs with my lifelong best friend, Sophia Rizzo. Donna was a year younger than me and a member of the local Presbyterian Church that was sponsoring us inner-city "underprivileged" kids for a week at summer camp. It cost $20 for the week, which might not seem like a lot but in those days was a week's worth of groceries. My parents and my grandmother had pooled their money and I was on my way. All I needed was the suitcase.

That night I felt a little cramp of anxiety in my stomach at the thought of it. I get the same little cramp today when I travel to unfamiliar destinations for the first time. The writer W. Somerset Maugham, quite the traveler himself, once said, "There are too many tourists and not enough travelers." I wanted to be a traveler. And this is exactly what I announced to my grandmother and my great-aunts the night we went to pick up the little red made-in-Italy *valigia*, suitcase.

I told them I wanted to go to Italy. No! Paris. Wait! First camp then Paris then Ireland to visit the other side of my family.

"*Madonne*. You already have a list," my Aunt Rosie laughed. She was fanning herself with a newspaper, her abundant jet-black hair tied up in a kerchief and her lips, as usual, impeccably painted in bright red lipstick. "Vi, what are we going to do with this child?"

Grandma Vi responded with a knowing look directed my way. "All you need is a place to hang your hat."

"Vi!" Aunt Josephine exclaimed. "You're going to make this child a gypsy talking like that. She'll never be home." Even on hot summer nights my Aunt Jo wore her long wavy brown hair loose so everyone could admire what she believed was her crowning glory.

"Careful, Vi," Aunt Justina warned as she rhythmically snapped the ends of green beans on the lap of her red-flowered housedress. Her ample bosom heaved with every breath. "It could be a blessing, but maybe not. What she does is up to God."

At that, they all crossed themselves.

I felt a little like Sleeping Beauty with her fairy godmothers arguing over the proper gifts to bestow upon her. As my great-aunts debated the various merits of which blessing I should have, my grandmother remained placid. Even then I knew she was wise; she knew what was best for me.

The conversation turned to my immediate destination: summer camp. Everyone seemed satisfied that at least this wasn't too far from home, but at the same time summer camp was a foreign concept to them. Until then, the farthest one of us children had travelled was to the local playground, and then with the strict admonition to be home when the streetlights came on.

"What's the name of this summer camp?" asked Aunt Mary, the youngest of the five sisters. She was dressed in white Capri pants and a modestly cut red halter-top, her hair pinned up on top of her head. Standing there, sipping her pink lemonade, she looked like a pin-up girl from a 1940s magazine.

I studied the group in front of me. The color red seemed to define my childhood, from my grandmother's glamorous nails, Justina's dress, Rosie's lips, Mary's halter-top and now the little suitcase. All of them were nothing if not passionate.

"It's called the Highlands and it's in Middlefield. It's Amish country," I answered, pleased with my knowledge of Ohio geography.

My aunts all looked at me like I was speaking an Italian dialect they didn't understand. Their world was limited to the west side of Cleveland from 117th Street to Public Square. Making a trip across town to the east side, to that "other" Italian neighborhood, was far enough for them. Beyond that, they would have packed bags.

"You go with who?" Justina wanted to know.

My grandmother headed off the question before I could answer. "The church," she said.

They all nodded their approval. I knew she wanted to leave it at that but I couldn't resist mischievously adding, "The Bethany Presbyterian Church."

Four pairs of eyebrows shot up in unison. They all turned and looked at my grandmother, who just shrugged.

"Eh," was all she said.

They all crossed themselves again. If there was a font of holy water nearby, they would have thrown me in it. All except my grandmother: she winked at me.

CHAPTER 2:
PINK CARNATIONS AND ELEPHANT SONGS

Since when did you become so Irish? —Mom

When I was growing up I sensed I was different than my six siblings, my 27 first cousins and most of my Italian–American school friends. It's not like I was a freak or anything; I was accepted and even indulged for my eccentric interests. "Oh that's just Cat," everyone would say if I showed up at school wearing a purple beret one day or an Aran sweater the next. How much of that was nature and how much was nurture was debatable.

My mother always believed that nature provided the clay while family and circumstances shaped it. She was quick to encourage and cultivate our talents and just as quick to dismiss her own. From my grandmother and, I suspect, from all the Brizzi women before her, she inherited what modern science now calls the creativity gene. She also inherited their tendency toward malapropisms.

"My daughter Cat has a photogenic memory," she'd brag to the other mothers at the PTA, and they would all nod, suitably impressed. It might have been the wrong word but it was the right context, and everyone seemed to get it.

My mother would attribute her creativity to necessity. My siblings and I were always presenting her with last-minute dilemmas. The all-night dollar store would have been a real boon to my mother, but I suspect it would have stifled her on-the-fly creative talents.

"Mom, do we have any green velvet ribbon?"

"Why?"

"Tomorrow's St. Patrick's Day and I have to wear something green."

At our school the lower-grade girls wore a standard uniform of blue plaid jumpers and white blouses and the older girls wore plaid skirts and vests. The boys wore blue pants, white shirts and ties. Conformity was the rule of the day. The dull and drab dress code meant there was no leeway for anything green other than a hair ribbon or a button-down sweater.

It was ten o'clock at night. My mother looked at my grandmother, who just shrugged.

"Since when did you become so Irish?" she asked.

"Since I decided that it's time to express the other side of my heritage."

As an eighth-grader at Our Lady of Perpetual Pain I felt it was time to work on my self-expression. I knew I was taking a risk because Sister Monica, paddle in hand, walked the aisles of her classroom regularly commanding a classroom of rebellious adolescents to "get back in your shells." My spirited best friend, Sophia, with her quick wit and smart mouth, often forgot and got whacked for her carelessness. Whacking in our neighborhood had nothing to do with the mob and everything to do with school.

Being part Irish and a redhead I also inherited a certain amount of natural rebelliousness—actually, a lot of rebelliousness—but it was important for me to be subtle about it. I practiced the art of hit-and-run rebellion and this new Irish attitude would be just the thing to drive Sr. Monica nuts while still respecting the norms of the school. Not only would my classmates love it, my mother would stand behind it.

"Please, Mom."

"Okay, okay. I'll think of something."

I hugged her and went to bed secure in the knowledge that she would work her magic overnight, like some little Italian leprechaun, and I would wake up not with a pot of gold but something green to wear to school.

The next morning I woke up to the most amazing sight. There, sitting on the kitchen table, were two corsages and two boutonnieres, one for each of her school-aged children. How did she do that? I wondered. Upon further examination I could see that the carnation-style "flowers" were made of layers of light pink toilet paper squares, the only color we had in the house at the time.

They were beautiful. The design was based on the flowers we used to see on wedding party cars parked outside a church on Saturdays in the 1960s and 1970s before weddings got so fancy. She had carefully folded each one and tied it in the middle with green thread to create a fan. Then she'd separated the layers and cut the edges with pinking shears. She'd finished each flower with a sprinkling of green food coloring in a random pattern. She'd tied two flowers together for the corsages and used single flowers for the boutonnieres. The pale pink color (so subtle it seemed almost white) served only to accentuate the green dye and make the little dots look like emeralds. Diaper pins would hold them in place.

When I walked into Mass that morning all thoughts of rebellion vanished, replaced with immense feelings of pride. Not only was I proud to be Irish but I was also proud of my mother and her handiwork. She could make something out of nothing and she made it look easy. Please God, I remember thinking, let me inherit that gene.

When it came to nurture, my salesman father, who worked in the grocery business, made sure to instill enough confidence in his brood so we'd be comfortable in any situation, whether it was meeting new people or speaking in front of a crowd of strangers. He did this by instituting "The Show," a nightly after-supper performance ritual in which the four older children, ages 5 through 14, got up to perform while the three young preschoolers looked on in happy amazement at the spectacle unfolding before them. To prove there was nothing to it, my father joined in. We were our own reality show, only we didn't know it. "This Family's Got Talent," my father would probably have called it.

Our stage was just in front of the television, and the nightly prize was one dollar. That was a lot of money in those days. Every night before the performance my father made a big show of taking a dollar bill out of his wallet and laying it on top of our large Magnavox console TV. It was always a new dollar, crisp and clean. He'd rub it between his thumb and forefinger to make sure there was only one. We coveted the prize, each of us fantasizing about what treats and treasures a dollar could buy us at the local dime store.

The winner was determined by applause. During dinner we'd each lobby our mother and grandmother so persistently and expertly it would make a Washington politician blush. As the oldest I went first and I usually recited a scene from a play, perfecting acting skills never to be used professionally but handy nonetheless. I was a modern-day Portia pleading her case before a jury:

"The quality of mercy is not strained. It droppeth as the gentle rain from heaven."

My mother would lick her finger, touch my temple and, making a hissing sound, draw her hand back quickly as if she'd burned it with a hot iron. "How did you ever get to be so smart? It sure wasn't from me."

That compliment was better than a dollar any day, since my mom was one of the smartest people I knew.

My brother Jimmy, looking every bit as Italian as my grandmother with his dark hair neat and clean in a crew cut and his shining, big brown eyes, sang the very sad Irish ballad "The Wild Colonial Boy." It's about an Irish immigrant who leaves his home in Ireland and travels to Australia, where he meets a tragic end. I could never figure out if Jimmy's voice cracked with the emotion of the song or because he had just turned 13 and was, according to my mother, "at that age."

Next up was my sister Margaret Mary, whose new bellbottom pants were quickly turning into floods. (The quintessential middle child, she inherited the tall gene from my Irish grandparents.) At ten years of age, and with an unruly mop of long brown bouncy spiral curls and big blue eyes, she looked like a gangly Shirley Temple. Dancing lessons would have helped her, but they were a luxury we couldn't afford and their lack never stopped her anyway. She was a master of improvisation.

And then there was Michael, a five-year-old redhead with blue eyes and an endless supply of jokes, some that made sense and others that did not. They at least made him laugh. And when Michael laughed he laughed with his whole body, and that made us laugh.

I'm not sure if there is anything better or worse than performing in front of the hoots and heckling of your own family. Who best to knock you down a peg or two but those people who know you best, who know your weak spots and who may want revenge for some previous day's transgression, like eating all the Oreos? Then again there's no better training ground for bouncing back and developing a thick skin—two essential life skills that have served all of us well.

"Hey Dad," Jimmy would yell during one of Margaret's dances. "You should make her register those arms as lethal weapons."

"Hey Jim," I would retort. "Maybe if you win the dollar you can get yourself some singing lessons."

I heard my mother sigh. So much for love and harmony, she'd say to my grandmother. "This is more like Friday night at the fights."

The last person to perform was my dad. Slight of stature and whippet thin with curly brown hair and bright blue eyes, he was a natural entertainer and storyteller. He also had a beautiful voice. He always sang a few lines of a rather silly song, an old playground rhyme called "Ms. Mary Mack," but he called it "The Elephant Song."

I asked my mother for fifty cents
To see the elephant jump the fence.
He jumped so high,
He reached the sky.
And never came back till the Fourth of July.

The applause from his adoring audience was thunderous. It was clear who the winner was this night and every night because we were all too selfish and stupid to support each other on a rotating basis. We were all eternal optimists who were certain that the next time would be our turn to win the dollar. In the end, even with no green in our pockets, it was our colorful childhood that made us winners.

CHAPTER 3:
THE RED WINDBREAKER

If you want to play the outsider, then do it with cool. —Dad

I fell in love with the French language at Claire Clancy's house one day. Mrs. Clancy was going through the mail at the little writing desk in the hall. I loved Mrs. Clancy. She was a tall, imposing woman who was never without a book in her hands. She always gave Claire and me books to read or told us important things, like "Girls, never leave the house without your lipstick because you never know who you'll meet at the bus stop." I was only ten years old but I've never forgotten that advice.

That day she was responding to a wedding invitation. I glanced over her shoulder and pointed at the elegant script that appeared at the bottom of the invitation: R.S.V.P. "What does that mean?" I asked.

She smiled. "I've always liked that about you, Cat. You're as curious as they come. It's French," she added. "And it means *Répondez S'il Vous Plaît*."

The way she pronounced the words sounded like music. I repeated them to her. "Very good, Cat," she said. "Spoken like a real Parisian."

That was it. I was hooked. I spent the entire summer at the Waltz Branch Library. I read each of the *Madeline* books three times. Their color-saturated illustrations convinced me that Paris was my city. It was the 1970s and I would watch reruns of *Hogan's Heroes* and try to imitate Corporal Louis LeBeau's French accent. I would sing the Nat King Cole song "Darling je vous aime beaucoup" or the Beatles' "Michelle." I would make up a string of words, just nonsensical phrases, to practice getting the accent down.

My siblings thought I was a thing possessed, like I was speaking in tongues. "It's French," I would explain. Unimpressed, they would return to their Barbie dolls and Tonka trucks.

"Au revoir," I would say as I left the house, grammar book under my arm, to sit in my favorite spot underneath on old oak tree in the backyard. There I could read undisturbed.

"What country is it this week?" my mother asked.

"Still France," I answered.

"You're nothing if not single-minded, Cat. Remember what I told you."

Frustration crept into my voice. "Yeah, I know, I know. Don't get married! See the world! How come you didn't see the world, Mom?"

"I saw your father first," she laughed.

"Don't you want to see the world?"

"Oh I will someday."

"Really? How?"

"Through your eyes."

"And how am I going to get there?" I was thinking about the $300 in my savings account.

"You're going to study hard, get a scholarship and go to college."

The year I turned 14 I started babysitting to save enough money to cover my first year's tuition at St. Agatha's Academy. My parents did what they could, but with seven kids in Catholic school all that tuition was a drain on their finances. The public school system was not an option no matter how hard I tried. "Listen Mom," I would say. "I was thinking if I went to Jefferson Heights High, I could save my tuition for a study abroad program in the 11th grade. I wouldn't have to wait for college."

"Absolutely not. You're going to get a first-rate education and it won't be at Jefferson Heights, I can tell you that. Those long-haired hippies and all the dope. No. You're going to St. Aggies."

"And pay for the privilege with my own money?" My tone was snarky.

"Well, if we could we would, but that's right, you're going to have to help."

"Who says I'm going to college anyway? I can just get a good job."

"Graduate from St. Agatha's first. After that the rest is up to you."

An all-girls school came as a culture shock to me. Most of the over 200 girls in my class had come from large middle-class suburbs or wealthier "exurbs" on the west side of Cleveland and with friends they had made in grade school. There I was: alone and miserable. My mother would say, "It must not be that bad if you're still there," implying I could make a change anytime to one of the other private girls' schools. The public school system was still not an option.

It didn't matter what school I chose. I'd still be the odd girl out because most of my grade-school friends attended Jefferson Heights. So I decided to reinvent myself with the help of my dad. I think he finally got tired of me coming home every night hating everything and everybody. "If you want to play the outsider," he said, "then do it with cool."

That weekend *Rebel Without a Cause* played on the cable network, and we watched it together. "Wow, that's exactly how I feel, Dad," I said. "I'm such an outsider. I'm not good at making new friends."

"So if you think it's so tough to break into a crowd, why not start your own, one friend at a time? If you want to be an outsider then do it with cool. How about I get you a red windbreaker?"

I could see the movie poster in my head. Dean leaning up against the wall in his famous red windbreaker, cigarette in one hand, the other placed carelessly on his hip. Distant, dangerous and unflappable, he symbolized cool the way Che Guevara had symbolized revolution.

"Can I take up smoking?"

"Not cool, Cat."

"Okay, okay. But I'll take the windbreaker."

"Divide and conquer, Cat," he went on. "Play to your strengths. Don't hide them, but don't show off either. Remember, it doesn't cost anything to be nice."

There was only one reason I stayed at the academy that first year, and it was Judy Zedowski. Every night of my freshman year I called her to say I wasn't coming back, and every night she talked me into one more day.

Judy also came from a working-class background; her father was a butcher and her mom was a housewife. Judy was Polish and, like me, came from a family of hugs and kisses. On Sundays Mrs. Zedowski served exotic dishes like pierogi, kielbasa and sauerkraut. Instead of Dean Martin or Frank Sinatra, we listened to America's Polka King, Frank Yankovic.

Judy was smart and dependable. She was a truly good person who worked as a candy striper at the hospital and who wouldn't know how to get into trouble if she tried. She had short brown hair with blond-frosted bangs and large square glasses. But the best thing about Judy was her laugh, which wasn't a laugh at all but more of a snort. When Judy laughed we all laughed whether something was funny or not.

"Ah c'mon, Cat. What would I do without you? You're not the only one from a small school. We gotta stick together. Why don't we get you involved in something? An activity?"

"Can you see me in a candy striper's uniform? That 'Little Miss Sunshine' yellow is definitely not my color. But it looks great on you," I added hastily.

"Not the hospital, you goof, the school. You're a good writer and everyone loves your poetry. Why not write for the paper?"

"Boring."

"I don't think so. You can liven things up and add a little color. How about doing feature stories?"

I hated to admit she was right. I needed to do more than go to school, and the occasional line of verse in the annual *Carillon Magazine* wasn't enough. I'd ignored my calling long enough. Writing was work but it was the only work I liked, which explained my lopsided GPA with an A in English and a D minus in Algebra. I took her advice, settled in and joined the staff of the school newspaper.

Over the next four years I chose girls from different crowds to become friendly with. I assembled such a mixed bag of friends that no one quite knew where to pigeonhole me. Suddenly coming from "that neighborhood" was cool to the girls from the inner-ring suburbs and mysterious to my more sheltered exurb friends. Tired of their own boys next door, they loved to troll my neighborhood for all those darkly handsome Italian–American boys who attended St. Paul's and Loyola, and I was always willing to introduce them.

One snowy December day the cafeteria was full of seniors too lazy to brave the snow for a fast-food lunch at McDonald's. Stew was on the menu again. As I walked toward my usual table I bumped into Amy Meyers, definitely an in-crowd girl. "Hey Cat, that article you did on the cafeteria food was really funny. Is it true they wouldn't serve you for a whole week after that?"

In the story I had suggested that, because the daily fare was so bad, why not go to an all–junk food menu. I offered ice cream soup as an appetizer, a deep-fried Mars bar as the main course and pizza for dessert, all washed down with diet pop. The cafeteria staff was not amused and neither was the paper's advisor.

"Jeez, Amy," I answered. "I don't know how these rumors get started." Actually I did, but I wasn't going to tell her. It just added to my cachet.

Out of the corner of my eye, I spied a small table off to the side with a sign that said, "Christmas Cards for sale, $1 a box. All proceeds to go to charity for disabled kids." A very soft-spoken Sally Jensen sat quietly at the table waiting for customers. Sally was tall, thin and elegant with very slow, deliberate movements. I figured she would either end up as a yoga instructor or a nurse.

"How's business?" I asked her.

"Quiet," she said. "Our fundraising hasn't been going very well lately."

"Really?" I looked around at a full cafeteria and mentally computed the net worth of many of my fellow senior classmates. "Did you ask any of the girls as they were walking in?"

Sally shrugged.

"Sales can be a tough gig. Girl Scout cookies and chocolate bars are all good, but Christmas cards…not exactly a big seller with this crowd. Here," I said, pulling a dollar out of my wallet.

"Thanks, Cat. You're my first sale of the lunch period."

"How many boxes of cards do you have to sell?"

"Thirty."

"Do you mind if I help?"

As Sally went to get another chair, I stopped her. "That's not exactly what I had in mind."

Her normally placid expression changed to a look of confused panic when I picked up the carton of Christmas cards.

"Judy!"

Judy crossed the cafeteria. I held out the box. "Here, take this and follow me."

"But, but," was all Sally could manage to say.

My first stop was the party-girl table.

"What?" Pat Moynihan barked at me, her pack of Kool menthol cigarettes bulging out of the breast pocket on her official school blazer. Pat was a study in contrasts—a petite girl with a big voice. She exerted a lot of influence in her crowd, but in time I would learn that her tough exterior was all show; inside she was a real softy.

I didn't know that then, so I was pretty brave when I asked, "How would you like to do a good deed and buy a box of Christmas cards to benefit a disabled kids' charity?"

"I don't send Christmas Cards," Pat said.

"Your mom can send them. Gimme a dollar."

"Why should I?"

"Because you're only going to piss it away on cigarettes and beer and then what will you have to show for it? This way you have an opportunity to do a good thing *and* have something to show for it."

Pat threw back her head to clear the straight blond bangs from her eyes. She gave me the once-over.

"Okay."

"And your friends too?"

"Huh?" A collective chorus of voices answered at once.

"What, do you think I'd let you guys forgo the opportunity to miss the one good deed that will get your sorry asses into heaven?"

And so it went with every table and every crowd. The girls with the least amount of extra cash gave the most. When I finally got to the "money" table, I couldn't help myself.

"Thank you so much. Unfortunately, there won't be any tax receipts with that contribution."

You could hear nervous tittering at the table as I walked away. I wasn't sure if they realized that the joke was on them. I placed an assortment of 30 one-dollar bills, wrinkled, crumpled and perfectly pressed, and eight boxes of Christmas cards in front of Sally.

"Wow, that's, that's... great! How come you still have eight boxes?"

"Pat Moynihan's group doesn't believe in Christmas. Here's an opportunity to make eight more dollars."

Sister Jean, one of the younger nuns at the school and our cafeteria monitor, walked over and pulled a dollar from her skirt pocket and handed it to Sally. "God helps those who help themselves."

Then she turned to me. "Good job, Cat. Next time, watch the language."

CHAPTER 4:
AN OLD GREY DODGE

You know, your sister would be really pretty if she only lost ten pounds and got her teeth fixed. —Carole Petrowski

She didn't have to say anything but I knew what my little sister was thinking. *We're late again.* As a ninth grader and in her first year at the academy, Margaret Mary was very keen to make a good impression. I, on the other hand, was on my way out; it was my last year, I was 18 and I couldn't care less.

We had just finished a breakfast of pancakes and hot chocolate at the IHOP up the street, effectively missing our first-period classes for the third time that month. I wondered how much longer I could blame our habitual lateness on bad driving conditions and distance. I knew I was pushing the limits of Sister Kevin's good humor.

Sr. Kevin, a sprite of a woman with hair the color and texture of steel wool, taught at the academy for 30 years until her hearing started to go. It was her eagle-eyed vision—she could spot a uniform violation at a hundred yards—that made her the perfect central hall monitor and attendance taker.

Stern but fair, she doled out detentions only if she thought you were abusing the system. And what teenager doesn't? If she didn't like you it could mean a couple of hours of detention a week, but if she liked you (and she liked me) she'd give you a free pass. She knew I worked after school and couldn't afford the detentions, but after four years the poor inner-city kid routine was wearing thin on her.

When I was a freshman I could blame my tardiness on the bus. "Sister, I was up all night studying and I didn't hear my alarm and missed the 6:00 a.m. bus. You know how it is living in the inner city. I have to take two cross-town buses just to get here."

Now that I had a car it was a bit more challenging to come up with excuses.

"Honestly, Cat; I don't know how you can lie with a straight face," Margaret Mary said. "We've run out of gas twice in the same week, and a spark plug exploded—which, by the way, I don't think is possible."

"Sr. Kevin doesn't drive. How would she know?" I replied.

Over the past two years I'd earned a good buck at the local grocery store. I'd paid my own tuition, expanded my record collection, bought some cool platform shoes and helped my little sister with her tuition. Senior year of high school, I was biding my time. I kept my head down, worked hard, got decent grades and stayed out of trouble. I had a good used car, a 1971 Dodge Dart—the "bondo-mobile," my brothers called it. It was dull metallic blue with battleship grey patches. It didn't look like much but it was reliable and good on gas.

I lived life on my own terms and I liked it. Grades, late slips or uniform violations, it didn't matter. I answered only to myself and the school knew it because the check I delivered every month to the administrative office had my name on it.

That snowy Monday, I winced as I skidded into the space next to Patty Tracey's bright red VW Beetle. I knew I should get the Dart painted but it would have to wait till I saved extra money. I put that on the list along with braces. There always seemed to be more pressing expenses.

We bumped into Kitty Bradstreet and some of the in-crowd coming out of the attendance office. They'd also stopped for breakfast at IHOP but Kitty's slip read "unexcused." Sr. Kevin's voice trailed after her: "One more unexcused late and it will go on your permanent record, Miss Bradstreet."

"I supposed you're excused again," Kitty said.

I held up the excused slip by the corner and dangled it in front of her.

"I guess there are certain advantages to being underprivileged, right girls?" Kitty laughed.

"Hey, watch it," Margaret said.

"I don't suppose you'll be joining us in Paris this spring?"

Kitty was the president of the French Club and visited France often. But her pronunciation was oh-so-American, and her vocabulary was limited.

"Malheureusement, je dois travailler pour payer mes études. Non, je suis très occupée," I said.

Kitty and her group walked away in a huff.

"Wow, what did you say? Margaret asked. "She looked mad."

"It's not what I said; it's the fact that she didn't understand a word of it. I just said I was busy."

I tugged on Margaret's elbow and rolled my eyes. "C'mon. Who cares what they think? Remember what Mom always says: It's not the clay; it's what you do with it. And we're going to do plenty, you and I."

My second-period class was advanced journalism. We were either working on articles for the school newspaper or the yearbook. This class could be so much more fun if we could report on things outside of school, I thought.

"Hey, Therese, what would you think about a feature called 'A Day in the Life at an All-Boys School'?"

Therese never-a-hair-out-of-place Kittredge was perfect. She was student council president and friends with everybody from nerds to party girls. She kept a case of hairspray, a sewing kit and a bottle of white shoe polish in her locker. It rained a lot in Cleveland and she felt it was important to be prepared. Her uniform pleats were razor-edge perfect and her blazer always looked like it just came from the dry cleaner's. When prospective students came for a visit, the good sisters always turned to Therese Elizabeth Kittredge to serve as a goodwill ambassador.

"I think it's a great idea, but Ms. McCain would never let you do that," Therese said, not bothering to look away from the paste up the board. She was trying to maneuver a column of type with an Exacto knife.

"How do you know?"

"No one has ever done anything like that before."

"So that's exactly the argument we're going to use. Are you with me?"

She didn't say anything. I nudged one of her pristine saddle shoes with my foot.

"Hey, I just polished these this morning!"

"Are you with me or not?" I asked.

"You're crazy."

"Maybe, but I need a prom date and this is the best way I can think of to meet some guys. Do you have a date?"

"No, but it's only January. We've got lots of time," she said.

"Right, and time's a wastin', so let's go."

Therese fiddled with the ends of her hair while I made my pitch to Ms. McCain. Dorothea McCain was definitely old school when it came to the newspaper. She had never worked at a newspaper but she managed to wring the best writing possible out of her students. Everything about her was severe, from her close-cropped grey hair and round wire-rimmed glasses to her conservative attire of "I mean business" pant suits.

I tried not to seem too eager or she'd suspect we were going after more than a story. As we stood there I swear I could almost hear her thinking, "the audacity of it all." Finally, she inhaled deeply and shook her head from side to side in disbelief. Out of the corner of my eye, I could see Therese's face fall.

Well, I thought. We tried. I thanked her for her time, grabbed Therese by the arm and was about to beat a hasty retreat when Ms. McCain cleared her throat. "Ladies!" She pulled a pencil from behind her right ear and wrote something on a piece of paper. It was permission for a one-day absence for us both. I stared at the permission slip for a long time before it registered that we had successfully negotiated a day off.

"Cat," she said. "I want a thousand words, and they better be good. Take the camera with you. And Ms. Kittredge, I want three sidebars from you on their student government, their newspaper and the pros and cons of having female students participating in classes."

"Yes, ma'am. Thank you, ma'am," Therese said.

"You won't regret it, Ms. McCain. I promise," I added.

"I'll be the judge of that."

Therese and I backed out of her office and ducked into the nearest lavatory. I looked under the stall doors; the place was empty. We grabbed each other by the shoulders and jumped up and down in a circle. We were going to spend a day at St. Paul's High School, one of the largest all-male Catholic high schools in Cleveland.

Therese left to catch her bus home. I stayed behind and ducked into one of the stalls to sit and think. I heard the door open, then the sound of voices: my sister's and Carole Petrowski's.

"You know, your sister would be really pretty if she only lost ten pounds and got her teeth fixed. She could get a boyfriend in a minute," Carole said.

"Wow! Really nice of you to be so concerned, Carole. I'll be sure and tell her, you being such a good friend and all. Or would you like to tell her yourself?"

"I didn't mean it like that."

"No, I'm sure you didn't. I'm sure you only have Cat's best interests at heart. If you want to be so helpful, why tell me? Why not tell her to her face, like maybe the next time she picks you up from the bus stop in the morning? You know what your problem is? You wish you were Cat."

I heard the door swing open and my sister stomp out into the hallway, with Carole following and calling after her.

I stepped out of the stall and examined myself in the mirror. It was true what Carole had said, but I'd never really given it much thought. Okay, snacking on the job might have caught up with me, but I could lose that weight if I wanted to. As for my teeth, the incisors were a bit high and pointy, but I couldn't afford braces and high school at the same time. I'd always thought I had a nice, easy smile.

It was also true that I had a lot of boy friends but no boyfriend. I chalked that up to the fact that I was busy with work, school and extra-curricular activities. I didn't have time for a boyfriend. Besides, I thought, there was more to a person than looks. I was smart and funny, and I was a good friend. Why wasn't that enough to get by in the world? Unfortunately, I knew why. People always noticed the new red Volkswagens and ignored old Dodges, cars that needed a little sprucing up no matter how reliable they were.

Only ten minutes before, Therese and I had jumped for joy in the john. We were going to spend a day at an all-boys school, which would put us well in advance of the prom date seekers who wouldn't even be thinking about lining up an escort for at least another two months. I had been quite pleased with myself, and until the moment Carole had walked into the john I'd felt I could do anything.

I leaned against the sink and looked at my slightly rounded face in the mirror. My thick, oversized glasses hid my blue-green eyes. The pixie cut I wore looked great on Mia Farrow but it didn't flatter me. The frosted bangs made it worse.

Was Carole right? I had the looks, I was sure of it. The clay, my mother liked to call it. But could I shape it into something beautiful? And how? Suddenly I no longer felt like going to St. Paul's in quest of a story or a prom date. I narrowed my gaze and squared my shoulders. I wasn't going to cry. I told myself it didn't matter and I would keep telling myself that until the day I believed it.

CHAPTER 5:
GOLDEN GLOVES / GOLDEN GIRL

What reporter in this tool and die town would ever seriously consider a boxing feature by a girl? —Cat

When I entered the house I could hear whispering and the clinking of china coming from the dining room. I peered around the corner and spied my mother pouring tea and my grandmother passing around a plate of Italian cookies to a group of elderly women. There were six of them—my father's aunts, my Irish great-aunts—sitting bolt upright, hands clasped demurely in their laps.

My Irish great-aunts never got old because they started out that way. Unlike my Italian aunts, who were youthful in their dress and attitude, these six ladies were serious and exigent. They looked nearly identical because they were all so close in age. Their uniform of choice was a floral print dress, cat's eye glasses, sweater, sensible orthopedic shoes and support hose, pillbox hat and gloves.

I turned away and collided with my nine-year-old brother, Danny.

"Who died?" I whispered as I grabbed his arm.

Danny wrenched his elbow free. "I don't know. Some old Irish guy. He's across the street."

The term "across the street" was code in our family for wakes held at the O'Leary Funeral Home opposite our house. It was a good location, within easy walking distance to both the Italian and Irish churches that made up the two overlapping neighborhoods. The Irish aunts made it a habit of dropping by for a cup of tea and a chat after a visitation at the funeral home. My father, who read the obituaries as regularly as he read the sports pages, was nowhere to be seen.

"Where's Dad?"

"He's at the zoo," Danny replied. "The zoo" was also code in our family for the racetrack. My father always saw a trip to the racetrack as a good opportunity to avoid social calls with his aunts. I put a finger to my lips.

"He took Bethie and Donna," my brother added.

BethAnn and Donna were my two youngest sisters, ages eight and six respectively. "I was out playing and I missed them." He kicked at the wooden floor. Covered from head to toe in mud, he looked like a pygmy in a flannel shirt and tennis shoes.

"Great, just when I need to tell him something."

"Did you do something wrong? Are you in trouble at school?"

"Not wrong, exactly. Can you keep a secret?"

He nodded.

"You know Lorenzo Fulmini, right?"

"You mean Lightning Lorenzo, the boxer? Your friend?"

"Yeah, that's right. He's got a very important fight on Friday night. It's the Golden Gloves Championship. I'm trying to make him a little more famous. I wrote a story and sent it to the *Cleveland Plain Dealer*. I want to get him some publicity, like the pros have."

"You're a girl. What do you know about boxing?"

"That's where Dad comes in. I signed his name to the story."

"Uh oh, you're in big trouble now."

"Hey, wait a minute, this is not like the time I signed my own report card. This is a good thing."

Danny shook his head and darted down the long hallway to the back door. "I still don't want to be here when you tell him," he called back over his shoulder.

I was about to follow him when I heard someone call me by my full name—Catherine Brigid. I was being summoned. As I entered the dining room I was overpowered by the collective scent of carnations. I wasn't sure if it was the aunts' perfume or the residual scent of funereal flowers. I hoped it was the former. I made the rounds and kissed each cheek.

"Whist now, there's she is, da lovely creature." I could never figure out how my mother or grandmother understood what the aunts said, their brogue was so thick. When they talked amongst themselves it sounded so much like a whisper, I couldn't quite tell if they were speaking English or Gaelic. "Shush, shush, shush, shush." And "mush, mush, mush." And then there'd be an occasional laugh or a disapproving headshake. My mother and grandmother would smile and nod. Somehow my grandmother always understood what they said. Perhaps it was because they were peers; they had lived through the same immigrant hardships. They shared what she would call an "understanding."

"You'll be finishin' with high school, now, I expect," Aunt Grania said as she took a long drag on her Pall Mall cigarette. I watched, fascinated, as she exhaled the smoke through her nose. She reminded me of an aging Hollywood starlet.

"That's right. In a couple of months."

"Den you'll be off to college, I presume?" Aunt Bridgie asked.

"I haven't made up my mind yet about college, but I do know one thing. I'm going to travel."

"Louisa, do you really tink tat's wise, a girl her age traveling alone?" Aunt Maureen wrung her hands with worry. "Imagine what could happen to her."

"Imagine," my mother said as she shot me an amused look. She worried about me more than the six of them combined but she couldn't do anything about her wayward daughter.

The conversation lasted another half an hour before the dishes were cleared and my aunts gathered up their sweaters and left. I could hear Aunt Moira commenting to Aunt Patricia on the way out, "Ah, our Jimmy did all right for himself. Dat Louisa, such a nice girl even if she is I-talian."

"Just wait till your father gets home," my mother said in a huff. "He always does this to me, and they're *his* aunts."

"I think he got home a while ago," I said. "His car's in the street. He's probably hiding in the den."

"I'll shoot him." My mother's deadly plans were interrupted by a booming voice from the den.

"Cat! Cat!"

"That would be himself," my mother said in her best imitation of an Irish brogue. "You best see what he wants."

I walked into the den and found my father at his desk, his hand over the mouthpiece of the telephone. "I have Craig Mayhew, the sports editor of the *Plain Dealer*, on the phone. Is there anything you want to tell me?"

"You're kidding! He's calling about Lorenzo, right?"

My father nodded. I pulled a carbon copy of a poorly typed news story on onionskin paper out of my purse and handed it to him. He pushed the handset against his shoulder and began to skim it.

"Honest to God, Dad, I meant to tell you. I wrote this about Lorenzo and his Golden Glove fight this weekend. It's a local angle, based on the movie *Rocky*."

My father nodded. "Good idea. And you sent it under my name?"

"What reporter in this tool and die town would ever seriously consider a boxing feature by a girl?" I was angry at the unfairness of it.

My father put up his hand to stop me, exhaled and shook his head. He took the call.

"They want to interview Lorenzo tomorrow," he said after he hung up, "and they want me to be there. Do you want to come along? It might be a good idea to fess up. You know, tell the truth and shame the devil."

I thought about it. I'd just placed my first story in a local newspaper. I wouldn't get a byline, but I didn't care. The fight would get covered and everyone in the neighborhood would know it was me.

"No. No, not a good idea. The editor might get mad and it might hurt Lorenzo's chance at publicity. It's okay. You go without me."

"You're sure?"

"Positive." I put on my game face and gave my dad a smile. I was balancing the mixed emotions of excitement and disappointment. I told myself there would be other opportunities. On my way out, I stopped in the doorway. I could see the smile on my father's face as he read the article.

"Oh, and Dad."

"Yeah," he said, not looking up.

"Paragraphs two and three are the best part of the story. Make sure he includes those."

My father stopped and laid the article on his desk. "Cat, you should really think about this writing thing. I mean, you're good at it. Really good. There are schools that specialize in this."

I hated to admit it but maybe he was right. I could have a job or I could have a career. It was my choice.

CHAPTER 6:

SILVER SPOONS AND JODHPURS

What's the worst that could happen? —Shelley Pembroke

Ohio University looks like it belongs on a movie set at Paramount. The federalist architecture, the mature trees, the brick streets and the main college green could serve as the perfect backdrop to many traditional American university campuses that came into being in the 1800s. The campus sits nestled in the picturesque landscape of southeastern Ohio's Hocking Hills. There's something magical about the place.

The university was in the charming town of Athens, named for the original center of learning in Greece. My dad was right; it also had one of the top journalism schools in the country. It was, I'm ashamed to say now, my third choice in colleges. I had listed the Community College first, followed by Cleveland State and then Ohio University. Since I wasn't serious about my third choice, I actually thought I wrote The Ohio State University. When it came time for my dad to sign the application, he noticed I'd written Ohio University. It was one of those unexplainable cosmic mistakes.

Now, I can't believe I applied to a school sight unseen. Back then, the school would remain a name on paper right up until the day I arrived in the scenic college town of Athens in the fall of 1978. I shared the three-hour ride and the cost of gas with Pat Moynihan. I never imagined she and I would attend the same college, let alone live next to each other in the same dorm. What were the odds?

We helped each other move into our respective rooms. "Here," she said, handing me a small wrapped box. "It's a dorm-warming present."

I was shocked by her thoughtfulness. "Really?" I unwrapped it and stared at what was inside for about two minutes before it sank in. It was a box of Christmas cards. We burst out laughing.

I set up my stereo, then made my bed with a new polyester bed-in-a-bag from Sears. It was a yellow bedspread with bright orange flowers. I carefully folded the hand-crocheted throw made by my grandmother and placed it on the end of my bed.

I hung up all my clothes and put the trunk and the little red suitcase under my bed. Last but not least, I hung my *Rebel Without a Cause* movie poster over my desk. I left the top bunk for my roommate, a girl named Dina from a place called Sydney, Ohio, who hadn't arrived yet. The early bird, I thought, gets the lower bunk. I hoped she was nice and wouldn't mind. After settling in, I hit the admissions office.

"What do you mean you want me to declare a major? I just got here," I said.

The admissions secretary blinked over the top of her drugstore bifocals. Her salt-and-pepper beehive hairdo was at least ten inches high. "Honey," she said in a slow drawl particular to southern Ohio. "You can always change it." She pulled a pencil from behind her ear. I could tell she was used to dealing with confused freshmen.

"Marketing," I said, wanting to be practical.

She put the pencil to paper and started to write slowly. Experience had taught her to do these things slowly.

"No, wait. Journalism."

She started again. This time I didn't interrupt.

She handed me a packet with my work-study assignment for Ellis Hall. I'd be working for the English and Foreign Language Departments.

From day one, I had a full academic and work schedule along with three part-time jobs. I was determined to make enough money to enroll in the study abroad program in France in my second year. I figured if I did the work-study job in the morning, worked as a part-time server at Jeff Cafeteria for lunch and sold advertising space to local merchants for the student newspaper, the *Post*, in between, I'd have the extra money to cover my travel expenses.

I don't remember much about my first year but I must have done some things right. Thanks to all my hard work, I also earned a partial academic scholarship and some extra cash for my trip. But would it all be enough? I'd soon see.

Year two was a reprise of year one: work and study. Spring finally arrived and with it my imminent departure date. I went to the bank to make a final deposit in my checking account. I glanced at my bank statement. All those hours spent working and I was still short. My heart sank. The fees had gone up and the cost of the program plus room and board was more than I had anticipated. Now I couldn't afford a direct flight to Paris; I'd have to find another way. Time was running out and I didn't have much money left over for extras. I also didn't want to delay my trip until my third year.

"We could arrange for a student loan," a sympathetic bank teller offered.

I shook my head. "I'd have no way of paying it back while I was in Europe." That was not an option.

"Do you have anything you could sell?"

"Sell?"

The large wooden fruit crate containing my entire record collection weighed a ton. I put it down on the pavement and pulled open the glass door to Bass Records, a local retailer on Court Street that bought and sold used vinyl. Using my foot as a doorstop I propped the door open and picked the crate back up. I looked down the dark stairway and sighed. Ziggy Z was never going to do anything about the bad lighting because it was part of a time warp, a sixties radical image he worked hard to preserve.

Ohio University's Athens campus was perched precariously on the edge of change, trying to decide whether it should hold on to its laid-back past or move on into a fast-paced future. The hippie/bohemian culture of head shops, peasant dresses and army jackets was slowly giving way to the newly emerging preppie culture of Oxford shirts, chinos and frat parties. Luckily, I experienced both. And like the majority of my peers in the early 1980s, I fell somewhere in between the two worlds; my eclectic record collection was a testament to that.

I was counting on Ziggy to fork over at least $150 cash for the collection in addition to a signed purchase order for a three-by-five-inch ad for the *Post* where I continued to work as a part-time sales rep. That sale would give me an additional $50 in commission. I mentally added my weekly earnings in my head.

I pushed the crate up onto Ziggy's counter. "Hey now, what do we have here?" he asked. Ziggy was a small man with round wire-rimmed glasses. He wore a red bandana headband and a salt-and-pepper hair braid that fell to his waist. He was one of the few remaining rebels who'd come to Athens in the 1970s, tuned in, turned on and never left. He was the last of his kind.

"My entire collection. Everything from Emerson, Lake and Palmer and James Taylor to The Police. No disco though," I added. "How much for the lot?"

"Buck each."

"What? You're offering only $1 each?! That's crazy. I have at least five albums here that are collector's items, autographed by the band members themselves. They're easily worth $10 each. One hundred and fifty."

"Sorry, Cat, no can do. Overhead is killing me. These landlords are capitalist pigs."

"But Ziggy, you're a capitalist," I said.

"A hundred bucks; take it or leave it."

"Well, it's not as much as I hoped for, but I'll take it. With some careful budgeting I should be fine," I said mostly to myself.

"When do you leave?"

"Sixteen days. After the break and then it's *bonjour la belle France*. Ten weeks in the Loire Valley. I told you I was going to study at the Institut de Touraine in Tours, right?"

"You told me at least 100 times, and half the campus too."

"Eh, what can I say?" I threw up my hands in an exact imitation of Grandma Vi.

Ziggy went into the back room and returned with the cash. "Here," he said as he counted out the cash. "And you'll be needin' this." He laid a purchase order on top of the pile of cash. I folded it and was about to stuff it into my jeans pocket with the cash when Ziggy stopped me. "Aren't you even going to check it out?"

I gave him a puzzled look. He'd been running the same ad for years. Why would I bother to check it? I pulled it out of my pocket.

"Oh Ziggy, are you sure? It's twice the usual size. What about your overhead?"

He just shrugged.

I ran around the counter and gave him a hug.

"Hey man, watch it, you'll wrinkle the flannel."

"Right, sorry," I said, smoothing down the already wrinkled front panel of his untucked shirt before turning on my heel to leave.

Ziggy stopped me when I reached the door. "Cat?"

"Hmmm?"

"Will you be going to Paris when you're there?" He didn't look up.

"Sure, sure I will."

"You know Jim Morrison is buried in Paris? In Père-Lachaise cemetery?"

"That's right."

Ziggy reached into his pocket and pulled out a crumpled bill. As he smoothed it out on the counter I could see it was $10. "Will you do something for me? Will you go say hi to Jimmy for me?" He handed me the bill. "I never had a chance to say goodbye."

Just when you think you know someone . . .

As I sat on the plane and watched my fellow passengers board the flight that would take us from Cleveland to JFK, I felt like I was watching myself in a movie:

Once upon a time there was this little girl who wanted to go to Paris and learn to speak French. Then one day the little girl grew up, sold everything she owned, bought a plane ticket and enrolled in French school in Tours, France.

As I sat there I felt very pleased and proud of myself and what I had achieved. I was going to learn the language and speak it like a native—pouty lips, Gallic shrug and all. I'd been working on perfecting my accent and expressions since I was nine and I played the part well enough to know I could pull it off. I would drink *pastis* in artsy cafés and pretend to smoke smelly Gauloises.

I fantasized about my ten-year high school reunion and the telegram I'd send:

Dear Girls (stop) Sorry I couldn't make our reunion (stop) Am living in Paris now working at Chanel (stop) Just couldn't get away as the fall collections are due out any day (stop) Bisou (stop) Catherine

I was so busy daydreaming about my new job as PR director at Chanel that it took a moment for me to realize that someone was calling my name. When I finally found my way out of my fantasy fog, I was able to place the voice and the face. It was Kitty Bradstreet.

"Cat! What a coincidence. I never meet anyone on airplanes."

I'd like to say that she looked exactly the same as she had at graduation two years earlier, but the truth was she didn't—she looked even better. Her blond hair was streaked to perfection, her skin was still clear and her teeth still straight and white. I self-consciously ran my tongue over my top teeth, feeling the difference in our smiles.

"It's so good to see you," she gushed. To hear her talk you would think we were long-lost friends. "You haven't changed a bit. I would have recognized you anywhere."

I looked up at her from the aisle seat like some supplicant addressing a goddess.

"Thanks. You look good, Kitty. You always did."

She was dressed in a little two-piece camel sweater set over wide-legged beige pants, and her shoes were adorable two-toned beige and black ballet slippers. But the pièce de résistance was her black quilted bag with gold chains and a double-C clasp. Chanel.

"Are you going to New York?" she asked.

"Yes. I mean, no. I'm in transit. I'm going to study in France," I said excitedly.

"Really? Me too."

My heart sank.

"I guess all those years as president of French club paid off," Kitty continued. "I've been studying at the Sorbonne since September."

I chose my next words very carefully. "Ah yes, the Sorbonne." I paused, then slowly added, "I've only just enrolled this spring for classes myself; I couldn't get away any sooner."

Well, it wasn't exactly a lie. Call it a sin of omission and ever so venial. I made a mental note to go to confession at Notre Dame when I got to Paris.

"Isn't that great! One thing's for sure, Cat, you won't have to worry about any late slips at the Sorbonne." She smiled sweetly.

Okay, so she wasn't so nice after all. "*I never* worried about late slips anywhere, Kitty." I returned the smile.

"Maybe we'll bump into each other sometime. Where are—"

I could see she was about to ask me where I was staying. I was sure she was staying near the Faubourg Saint-Honoré or somewhere swish like that. Thankfully, the buildup of human traffic in the aisle behind her pushed her forward.

"Let's catch up on the Air France flight over to Charles de Gaulle, okay?"

"That would be great. We'll chat then," I said with a hint of relief in my voice.

The reality was that I wouldn't be on the Air France flight from New York to Paris. I was flying Sabena, the national Belgian airline to Brussels, then taking the train to Paris. Lucky for me I was sitting at the front of the plane, which meant I disembarked ahead of her.

I had been in Paris all of three hours, just enough time to change trains from le Gare du Nord to le Gare Montparnasse to catch my connection to Tours. As I glanced down at my map of Paris I noted all of the little illustrations scattered about the city—the Eiffel Tower, the Louvre, Notre Dame—yet I wouldn't have time to see any of them. Orientation was the next day, and the school expected me there for a full briefing. I took comfort in the fact that once I settled in I'd be back to Paris the next weekend. Perhaps I could drag my roommate with me.

I pulled a neatly folded piece of customized stationery out of my pocket and looked at the coat of arms across the top: Oxford University. On the paper was a very polite note of introduction from my roommate, Shelley Pembroke. How very British, I thought as I flipped open the top of my backpack and took out a teddy bear with the initials "OU" stitched on its sweater. I hoped she would like it.

She did.

The only child of a Thai mother and a British father of title and wealth, Shelley possessed a Zen-like composure, a sharp mind and a natural athleticism. I tried very hard to hate her, but it was impossible; she was the world's best roommate. Men would fall at her feet by the dozens, and because there were always so many, she never minded sharing. Besides, her steady boyfriend lived in London so it would have to be a double date or nothing. I was her unofficial chaperone, her conscience, there to protect her from the spells of charming French men.

I looked over at Shelley as she reclined on her twin bed, paging mindlessly through her grammar book. Easter Monday in Tours and we were both bored because nearly everything was closed except for the riding stable at the end of the street and the local cinema. Studying all day was not an option.

"Let's go riding, Cat!" Shelley sat up, full of energy.

"No way," I said. "I can't ride. I grew up in the city. The closest I ever got to the country was when my dad took us to the stockyard to look at the cows."

"How sad."

"Oh it wasn't that bad. It wasn't exactly the country, but it was still an outing."

"I wasn't talking about you, Cat. I was talking about the cows."

We burst out laughing.

"Seriously, Shell. You were born in jodhpurs and boots."

"Don't forget the silver spoon."

"Oh yes, mustn't forget the silver spoon. I say we go to a movie. There's a new one with Meryl Streep and Dustin Hoffman, *Kramer vs. Kramer*. Looks good."

"It's a shame to waste such a beautiful day in a dark theatre. We can both take a lesson. I haven't ridden in years and it would be something totally new for you. You can go to a movie and you can ride like a cowboy in that big country of yours anytime, but how often can you say you rode equestrian style in France?"

She did have a point, but…"Them's awful big horses, pardner," I said in my best John Wayne.

"Come on, give it a try. What's the worst that could happen?" Shelley asked innocently.

Two surgeries and one week later, I was back with my host family, my leg propped up on three pillows. It seemed like my only souvenirs from France would be the stainless steel plate and nine screws keeping my ankle together.

"I'm sorry, Cat. I never thought that horse would throw you," Shelley said.

"It's not your fault—even if it was your idea." I threw a pillow at her.

"Can I bring you back anything from Barcelona?"

"Yeah. A cute Spaniard."

"I'm not sure Madame Colbert would go for that."

"Please, I'm practically family. I'm sure it will be fine."

Shelley kissed me on each cheek, left, right and left again for good measure. "See you Monday."

"Yeah, see ya."

"Cat, if it's any consolation, your French has really improved. This may have just been your lucky break." She picked up her backpack and left.

Easy for Shelley to say. But what if she was right? Housebound for the next six weeks I had nothing else to do but immerse myself in the day-to-day routine of my host family, absorb the culture and practice my French. Still . . .

I pounded the pillow on my twin bed. Why me? Why now? Oh, maaaaan. No Paris! No France! No Eurail adventures for me!

My cast didn't weigh as heavily as my disappointment.

CHAPTER 7:
RED O'MALLEY

Ma! There's a couple of Yanks at the door. —Cousin Moira

I started my third year at Ohio University in a subdued mood.

"Is everything okay, Cat?" friends would ask.

"Yeah. Sure. Fine," I'd reply.

The fact is that with my French trip a total disaster, I'd lost all of the exuberance of the previous year. Eventually I decided to take a more pragmatic approach and start working on my major, the tenth one since registering in the journalism program. I went from magazine feature writing and foreign correspondence to public relations and radio/TV broadcasting and back again. I finally settled on advertising. I already sold ad space for the *Post*, so advertising felt right. I pictured myself working for a big Madison Avenue agency and living in Manhattan.

College life careened between work and study, with an occasional social outing in between. I didn't date very much because most of the guys I liked weren't interested in me. And the guys who liked me, well how dare they think I'd even be remotely interested in them. My "lucky break," as I jokingly called it then, had added another five pounds to my petite frame, and like most young women my age facing the same challenge, my self-esteem went down as my weight went up.

I became the official best friend of every guy I liked. I was the go-to girl for advice, introductions and, if I really liked him, the occasional ghosted term paper. In return I got a few crumbs of attention from a good-looking guy like Jeff Bouchard, a handsome hockey player who lived next door.

Jeff looked and moved like a lion, from his tawny mane to his golden eyes. There was something cat-like about him. On the ice he was a predator looking for openings that didn't exist until he found them. Off the ice he prowled the campus practicing his charms on all the girls except me.

One afternoon I fixed my hair, made up my eyes and put on a skirt. I changed accessories six times; first a scarf, then a necklace, then a ribbon for my hair. I caught a glimpse of myself in the hallway mirror. I didn't look half-bad. I just wished I looked good. Jeff was on his way to pick up a term paper I'd helped him with.

"Cat, you're the best, really," he said when he got there. "Thank you so much for typing this paper for me." Typed, I thought. I also wrote almost all of it. I'm sure he meant to say that too. "Here, I got you something," he added.

I was touched and surprised. I took the small bag he was offering. It was definitely an article of clothing. My imagination ran wild with the anticipation of something soft and feminine. Maybe a pair of gloves?

I opened the bag and pulled out a hockey team scarf in the traditional green and white colors. A hockey scarf. It would have been better if he hadn't given me anything. I swallowed my disappointment. "This is, uh, very thoughtful of you. Thanks Jeff."

"Don't mention it, Cat," he said as he kissed me on the top of my head and turned to go. He paused at the door. "You look good tonight. Your eyes are very sparkly. Are you holding out on me, Cat? Are you in love?" he teased.

I blushed and looked away.

"I knew it! Well, whoever he is, he's a lucky guy, that's all I can say." After he shut the door behind him I leaned forward and banged my forehead quietly against it a couple of times. Silly girl, I said to myself.

Working for Sammy Lindeman, the yearbook editor, was much more enjoyable and, it would turn out, more satisfying.

Sammy stood barely five feet three inches tall; his clothes always looked two sizes too big and like he'd slept in them. Attempting to appear older and be taken more seriously by his peers, he kept an unlit pipe on his desk, tried to grow a beard (though succeeded only in sprouting a wispy mustache) and wore Old Spice. Something of a wunderkind, he'd entered college at age 16. Whenever I entered his office I was assaulted by the combined odors of sweat, aftershave, old coffee and sweet cherry tobacco.

"Hey," he said on one occasion.

"Hey."

"Remember that story you did last year on those Norwegian guys?"

"The swimmers?" How could I forget? I thought. I'd interviewed four of them, all incredibly tall and handsome in that square-jawed, Nordic sort of way that made me feel like I was standing in the middle of a forest. Damn me if they didn't look like real-life Vikings. Right then and there, I made a mental note to put Norway on my list of countries to visit someday.

"There's some sort of reciprocity program with the University of Oslo. It's for summer school. You interested in going?" Was Sammy offering me a second chance at Europe?

"Can't afford it. Blew all my money last year on France. I've run out of things to sell except maybe my body." I plopped down in the chair in front of his desk.

"The medical school is looking for simulation patients."

"Ha ha. I hear there's an open mike night at the Frontier Room for comics."

"You should know from funny." He turned serious. "Look. Let me worry about the money. There's a partial scholarship, and I'm sure we can work out a loan or something with the bursar. This is your last year so you won't have to pay it back until after you graduate."

Jan O'Neil, Sammy's business manager, looked up from her work at the mention of the Norwegian swimmers. Jan peered at us through her oversized glasses, her hazel eyes dancing mischievously. Her long wavy hair was piled on top of her head in a loose knot. Two number 2 pencils held it in place geisha style. She had CEO written all over her.

"I read your article. Those are some fine-looking specimens. There ought to be a law against men that good-looking," she said in an Appalachian drawl. "Speaking of breaking a few laws, would you like a partner in crime? I'd love to join you."

"You want to go to Norway?"

"Why not? It will look good on my resume."

Sometimes the best-laid plans don't always work out the way they're supposed to. That doesn't mean I can't have a new plan, a different plan. Maybe this time, I'd just show up.

"Okay, you're on, Jan. What's the phrase? Carpe do it?"

"Something like that," she said.

We shook on it.

A couple of weeks later after some hastily concocted financing, we were ready to go. We were headed for the library to pick up some books on Norwegian history when we saw the Norwegians playing Frisbee on the college green.

"Go on, Cat," Jan said, nudging me in their direction. "Say something. Tell them we're going to be in Oslo this summer. Maybe we can meet up."

I hesitated.

"Come on, isn't that what you do? Public relations? Go and relate," she urged.

I looked down at myself, casually dressed, wearing no make-up and sporting oversized glasses. This was not my finest hour.

"Next time."

Suddenly a Frisbee landed at my feet. I bent down to pick it up, and when I rose I was staring into a pair of glacier-blue eyes. It was Knut, the anchorman in the 400-meter relay. The sun shone behind him, creating a halo about his already golden head. He looked like a Norse god. I handed him the Frisbee rather than look foolish with a lame toss.

"Takk for det," he said, smiling.

"You're welcome," I said.

Jan grabbed my arm and pulled me toward the library and out of earshot. "Oh my God, oh my God. Did you see that? Do you think they all look like that? Boy, Cat, it's going to be a great summer."

It sure was going to be a great summer. I promised myself that this time I would keep both feet firmly planted on the ground. I would travel as God intended: by foot, in a car, on a tram or on a train. Once we had our fill of Norwegian language, music, art and, of course, herring, our plan was to strike out on our own and explore the rest of Europe. I composed a mental checklist of cities to visit. I figured out everything except how to tell my parents I would be going to Norway for the summer.

"Norway? We don't even know anyone in Norway. You've never mentioned Norway before," my mom said. She glanced over at my father who was hiding behind the sports pages. "Are you going by yourself?"

"No, no. I'm going with the yearbook business manager, Jan O'Neil. We've arranged for scholarships and loans to cover most expenses. And I plan to work when I get there."

"If you want to study in Europe again, why not pick a place where we have some family, like Dublin or Naples? Go somewhere where someone can keep an eye on you. You remember what happened the last time."

Remember? I'd be 50 and she'd still remind me. How could I forget? The souvenir stainless steel plate was bolted to my tibia.

"Your father and I were sick with worry last year. Weren't we, Jim?"

My father looked over the top of the paper and nodded. He was not going to get involved.

"Jesus, Mom, I'm 21. And I didn't do too badly looking after myself on crutches. I made it all the way back home on my own and with luggage. I promise I won't do anything experimental this time."

During the never-ending Scandinavian summer days, Jan and I attended concerts featuring Greig and plays by Ibsen. Visits to the Munch Museum later inspired us to imitate the iconic subject of *The Scream* every time something went wrong. The plus-sized statues at the Vigeland sculpture park actually made us feel skinny. We explored the length and breadth of Oslo, but the one thing we never saw were the swimmers. It hadn't occurred to us that they would be off competing in swim meets throughout the whole summer.

Later that summer, our stint in Norway behind us, Jan and I sat on a bench in Hägas Park in Stockholm, an unfolded map of Europe between us. It was filled with red dots of all the places we wanted to visit: Copenhagen, Amsterdam, Brussels, Paris, Rome and the final destination, Achill Island, County Mayo, Ireland. We figured by the time we hit Ireland we'd be out of money and would throw ourselves on the mercy and legendary hospitality of my theretofore unknown Irish cousins.

We arrived at this conclusion because, chronologically speaking, I had more recent ties to Ireland than Jan. Her family had arrived in America over 100 years earlier whereas my family had been there a mere two generations. As with my mother's family in Italy, we still "knew people" in Ireland.

Jan thought it was a brilliant idea, "brilliant" being a word she had picked up from a couple of Brits on the train ride to Stockholm.

"Cat, you got family in Ireland, right?" she had said.

"Yeah, but Jan, I've never met them. They don't know me from Aiden."

"Isn't your godmother from there? Can't you call her and get a name or something?"

Realizing the practicality of her plan, that's exactly what I'd done. I'd called my Irish godmother, the aunt who still spoke with a soft Irish lilt and who told me stories of pirates and treasure. The aunt who sent postcards and brought me presents whenever she came back from a visit "over there."

My godmother had given me a name and an address. It wasn't so much an address as a place—Dereens Road—located on a sparsely populated island called Achill off the wild west coast of Ireland.

"But there's no house number," I'd said. "How in the world am I supposed to find it?"

"Not to worry," she'd said. "Just find the road. The rest will take care of itself." Like magic, I'd thought. Throw in a couple of leprechauns and a pot o'gold and this could be *Finian's Rainbow*.

"What do I say?"

"Tell them who you are." My aunt's voice had crackled across an underwater phone cable. "Tell them you're Catuaille's granddaughter. They'll know ya."

She pronounced my grandmother's name, Caitríona ni Máille (*cotch-treema-ni-woll-ya*), the old Gaelic way. Caitríona (Catherine) was the one who had left everything to come to America, the grandmother who had died before I was born and who I was named after.

I'd repeated the name like a mantra, Caitríona. It meant home, family and a safe harbor after a long and adventure-filled journey.

"Hungry?"

Jan's question pulled me back to the present and the prospect of lunch in this lovely little park. She pulled out a couple of peanut butter sandwiches and a bag of chips from her backpack. We lived on peanut butter that summer. Peanut butter and flatbread crackers; peanut butter and baguettes; peanut butter and ciabatta; peanut butter and chips, crisps and chocolate tablets.

Jan started to throw some of her bread to a few stray pigeons. "I don't think that's such a good idea," I said. "They may have lots of hungry friends."

"Nah. Besides, someone has to feed the animals. Frances is my middle name, you know. I could have been Francis of Assisi in another life."

"Well, in this life, St. Jan Frances, I think the word has gone out and your feathered friends have invited some guests."

"Oh shit."

Before we could stand and pack our things, we were surrounded by pigeons, what looked like thousands of them, although I'm sure there were only a few hundred.

"Cat, do something!"

"Why me? You're freakin' St. Frances. Perform a miracle. Multiply some loaves or something."

"But you're a city girl. I grew up in the country. You grew up with pigeons. You're used to things like this."

"This is like Hitchcock's *The Birds*," I said, the idea adding to our terror.

I stood and threw my sandwich into the middle of a grassy plain, which startled the pigeons and a few amused Swedish onlookers. As the pigeons scattered I grabbed my country-girl roommate and we ran for our lives, the echo of laughter dogging our steps.

We covered so much territory that summer, it was sometimes hard to remember where we were. "Where are we today?" Jan would ask.

"Marseilles," I said.

"I'm losing track of time and place."

"Yeah, isn't it great? A different city nearly every couple of days."

"When's the next train?" Jan asked.

"In 20 minutes."

We walked down the long platform until we saw an empty bench and parked ourselves there to wait.

"I can't believe you have us staying in a convent in Rome of all places. Have you seen those Italian men?" Jan asked.

"The ones with or without the gold chains? My mother always says if they're wearing conspicuous jewelry, they've got no money. They've spent it all on the gold."

"What if the convent has a curfew? We'll get locked out."

"And your point is...? It's Rome and it's night. Do we really want to sleep? Didn't you ever see the movie *Roman Holiday*? We can alternate our sleeps: some days, some nights. Nothing gets broken this way," I said, noticing a young dark-haired, sloe-eyed man. He approached and sat down next to me. He was well dressed and looked to be a few years younger than us. He began reading an Italian newspaper.

He greeted me in Italian and I returned the greeting. I quickly added that I didn't speak much of the language and that I was more comfortable in English or French. He switched to French.

"What's he saying?" Jan asked.

"His name is Giulio. He lives in Italy but spends the week in Marseilles working at the port. I guess jobs are scarce in the region he comes from. He's going home for the weekend."

Giulio gave me a meaningful glance, whispered in my ear, then leaned out and looked at Jan and smiled.

I felt my whole body flush. My face turned bright red.

"What did he say?" Jan asked as I pulled her to her feet and steered her down the platform.

I took a deep breath and exhaled slowly. For all our talk about men and relationships, Jan and I still didn't have all that much practical experience.

"He said Italian men make love twice a day."

"No!"

I nodded. "And then he said since there are two of us . . ." I let my voice trail off.

"What did you say?" Jan asked.

"I told him we're on our way to a convent in Rome."

Many red dots later we found ourselves at a café that looked out on both the Seine and Notre Dame Cathedral. Finally, I thought, I'm in Paris sitting at a café and sipping lemonade. This is where I belong. If only I could live and work here.

"Cat, I think we just broke the bank. The bill comes to the equivalent of $12."

"What, are you sure? For two lemonades?"

She gave me her best "I am the accountant" look and nodded.

"How much do we have left?"

"About $12."

"What do we have for food?" I asked.

"Half a jar of peanut butter, half a pack of Belgian chocolate, some gouda cheese and a few tea bags."

"Time to go."

"Time to go," Jan agreed.

She arranged to pick up an Amex money transfer in Dublin. It gave us just enough to complete our travels and get back home without having to commit any crimes or starve in the meantime.

"Are you sure this is the right train?" Jan glanced around at the different tracks in Dublin's Huestan railway station.

"There's only one and it's going to Westport."

"And then what?"

"There's a bus that takes us over a bridge to the island. We just give the driver the name of the road and we're all set."

"Sounds pretty straightforward."

When it comes to travel in Ireland we learned nothing is straightforward. We arrived in Westport during the dead of night and couldn't find a hotel. Luckily we met three cute French guys on the train who offered us a night in their tent at a local campground. They were much better prepared than we were when it came to travel, especially roughing it.

"I'm not sleeping with them," I whispered to Jan while they started to make camp.

"Me neither. We hardly know them," she whispered back.

"American girls," they laughed amongst themselves as they continued to set up the tent.

"We said in the tent, not with us," the one called François laughed. His curls bounced as he shook his head. "We'll stay outside in our sleeping bags. You don't have to worry."

"Typique," Patrick added to no one in particular.

"Hey," I said, offended, my hypocrisy showing.

"But if you get cold . . ." Yves added, flashing a sweet smile. His long black hair was tied back in a sexy ponytail.

That night we froze our asses off while three of the best-looking Frenchmen in the world slept cozily outside our tent in their sleeping bags.

We woke up early the next morning to catch the 7:00 a.m. bus to Achill. We gingerly stepped over the sleeping Frenchmen so as not to wake them. Jan placed the half-eaten box of Belgian chocolates and a note next to François. We walked briskly to what looked like a bus stop, rubbing our limbs to regain the feeling we'd lost sleeping on the cold, hard ground.

"There it is." Jan waved her arm to make sure the driver saw us.

"It's not like he's going to miss us," I said.

We were surprised to find the rickety red bus half-full of all sorts of people, produce and packages. I asked the bus driver how long we had to go before our stop and followed Jan to the back of the bus. As we settled in our seats, the bus made its way in a leisurely fashion down a blacktop road. There must have been 40 shades of green dappling the landscape. Jan interrupted my reverie.

"How long before our stop?"

"The driver says we should be there in about thirty—" I didn't have time to finish my sentence because just then the bus came to a screeching halt and the windshield popped out.

There were cows crossing the road in front of the bus. It was a Holstein parade and we stopped to let them file past. It took forever. "Hey Jan," I joked, "you're a country girl. Why don't you go out there and shoo them or something."

The driver hopped out of the bus, picked up the window and snapped it back in place. Our fellow travelers scarcely noticed the interruption in their journey. Jan and I looked at each other, wide-eyed. "Go Greyhound," Jan giggled.

We arrived at a crossroads, and the bus stopped at the top of the Dereens Road. There were no street signs or signs of life anywhere. To the left and right of us lay vast green fields broken up by the ubiquitous stone walls one sees everywhere in Ireland. Behind us was the sea.

The driver beckoned us forward. "There now, you'd be looking for the O'Malleys and they're just up the road a ways."

"How far is that?" I asked. The road looked like it stretched into infinity.

"Ah sure now, it's just up the road a ways. Not far at'all."

We walked for an hour without seeing a soul. The road was devoid of men, machines and animals. Occasionally a seagull flew overhead. We were getting desperate when a car rounded the bend behind us.

"Stick out your thumb, Cat. Let's see if we can hitch a ride."

"Why me?"

"'Cause you're a city girl. You're used to doing these things."

I was about to argue but I didn't want to miss the opportunity for a possible lift with this passing car. I figured there were fewer chainsaw murders here than in Texas.

"Cat?" Jan started as I boldly stuck out my thumb at the oncoming car.

"Yeah?"

"I was thinking about that big Irish family of yours. There's got to be at least a couple dozen Cats, Kates, Cathleens, Catherines."

"Probably. Why?"

"Think how confusing it will be when someone says 'Cat' and y'all answer."

"You worry about the darndest things."

"I just like to keep things neat and tidy. I think from now on I'm going to call you Red for your hair. Red O'Malley. Think about it, all of those red dots on our map and that little red suitcase I've heard so much about. It's perfect. What do you think?"

"I think it's very Katharine Hepburnesque. I like it."

The car pulled to a stop in front of us. Inside was a middle-aged couple from Belfast going to visit their own family near the O'Malleys. No, they didn't know them, but they knew where the house was. And sure they'd be happy to give us a lift.

"Jan O'Neil," my friend said as she stuck out her hand in introduction. "And this here"—she nodded her head in my direction—"is Red. Red O'Malley." She drew out the sound of my last name.

A few minutes later, Jan and I stood in front of a whitewashed, two-storey cottage. I rang the doorbell. No answer.

"Maybe they're not home."

"We would have seen them on the road," I said as I rang the bell again.

Above us we heard a casement window sliding up its well-used track. A young, dark-haired woman with bright blue eyes poked her head out the window and looked down at us. She then yelled back into the house, "Ma! There's a couple of Yanks at the door."

And with those words we were home. The next three days on Achill Island were the highlight of our trip. *Cead Mile Failte* (kaed meela fault-yih) means 100,000 welcomes in Gaelic, and welcome we were. We ate, slept and drank tea by the gallon. We spent our days admiring the savage beauty of the land and our nights in the local pub, singing and telling stories.

The day before we left, my cousin Paddy took me on a little tour of the island. Broad-shouldered Paddy O, never without a smile or a story. When he smiled his eyes crinkled and his dimples deepened into creases. He spent most of his years outdoors working the land, and it showed. Like all of the O'Malley cousins he towered over me. I took three steps to his one to keep up as we crossed the grassy knoll.

"See that. 'Tis all that's left of your grandmother's house."

I looked at the stone ruins at my feet. The surface area was just one large room. I couldn't imagine that small house—a hut, really—as home to five children and their parents. It was both humble and humbling. I imagined my grandmother growing up there, the only place she ever knew for 18 years. I marveled at her courage. She had crossed an ocean with the clothes on her back and a few pounds in her pocket in the company of her older sister. She had left behind her mother, father and three brothers for the promise of something better.

The Irish cousins spoke in hushed whispers of her heroic struggles in America to work, keep food on the table and find shelter for her young family of six. Finally, there was her last battle with breast cancer. No matter, her letters had always been bright and full of optimism. It was the neighborhood gossips back in Cleveland who had told her real story of hardship and deprivation when they wrote, "I hear Seamus lost another job. 'Tis the drink." "I hear they're parceling out the children to his sisters." "They removed the breast but she's still got the cancer." And so on.

"When we heard she was sick," Paddy said, "her brother took his bicycle and rode all day and into the night to the other side of the island to visit a wise woman, a healer. And he came back with a charm for her to wear. We sent it off to America with our prayers."

"And did it work?" I felt stupid for asking a question I already knew the sad answer to.

"Prayers are always heard, no matter the outcome. Have faith in God, who has faith in you. And now here you are. And sure'n she'd be proud that you're here having come all the way from America on your own and so much like herself. As brave as can be."

They say pilgrims come to Ireland to find God. I went in search of a little hospitality and a connection with my family. What I also found was steadfast courage and simple faith.

"I'm not brave, Paddy. But someday I hope I can live up to her kind of courage and your kind of faith."

DESTINATION: SHANGHAI

"Cat, I really appreciate you coming all this way to do these training sessions," Laura said as she checked her briefcase. It was her fifth time counting the training manuals she'd printed the day before.

"It's always great to see you and it's not often I get to Asia, so that's a bonus."

Laura Wong, my Chinese counterpart, sells color-merchandising tools in the Asia-Pacific region for our company. She's a petite package of compressed energy and wicked wit. Any opportunity to co-present or travel with her is always an adventure.

Our taxi dodged in and out of Shanghai traffic like a hummingbird. I grabbed Laura's arm. "We're going to die," I said.

"You'll get used to it."

"And I thought Manhattan cabbies were bad. Tell me again why I'm here risking my life?"

"Basically you're the new Western girl in town. I need a guest lecturer, someone with an outside perspective. Sometimes people stop hearing or seeing me, or maybe they take me for granted."

"Sounds familiar."

Laura studied me from under the fringe of her asymmetrical auburn bangs.

"Hey, that hair color looks great on you," I said. "Speaking of color, tell me about the audience."

"Smooth, Cat, real smooth."

"Thanks."

"Well, as you already know they're one of the largest paint companies in Asia, and Shanghai is a growing market." Laura opened her arms in a sweeping gesture that took in the dense jungle of ultra-modern architecture that surrounded us. East meets West in a dizzying blend of steel and glass.

The night views took my breath away. My head was still swimming from the sensory overload from all the neon on the Nanjing Road where we had eaten dinner the night before. I had felt like I was inside some giant cosmic kaleidoscope. The colors changed constantly as I turned in circles, taking it all in.

"This morning we're talking to sales associates in two of their largest stores," Laura continued. "It's primarily a female audience and corporate wants to train them to sell color."

"If you can sell color, you can sell paint. Corporate has the right idea. My presentation covers color theory and color scheming. And I've added some selling techniques, like identifying wants and needs and reading body language. Is that okay?"

"Perfect. I'll finish off with Asian trends."

Once at the store we set up the training area in the back. Employees were preparing tea and setting out *pinyin,* Chinese cakes. We had eaten breakfast at the hotel, but the scent of warm almond cookies, moon cakes and cream buns set my stomach rumbling.

"Go on, take one. You can always blame it on jet lag," I heard a voice say from behind.

I turned to see Margaret Chen smiling broadly at me. Margaret, corporate marketing director and initiator of the training program, shook my hand warmly. We'd met some months before at a color conference in Seattle. She was dressed smartly in an eclectic mix of Vuitton and Anime. Her signature LV bag and shoes were paired with a brushed silver jacket over flared satin pants, topped with a wide red belt.

"If I had your perfect figure, Margaret, I might be tempted," I responded. "But all of that delicious red bean paste will go right to my middle."

"I wouldn't worry about it, Cat. We have a tight schedule over the next three days. You and Laura will be running between appointments."

"*Now* you tell me," I said as I raised my basic black pant leg and rotated my foot.

"Nice Louboutins."

"In the latest trend color, quite possibly the only thing trendy about me."

"On that note," Laura interrupted, "we're ready to start."

I gave a brief overview of color theory, spectrum and wavelengths. I didn't want to bore my young audience with too many details, so I soon switched to the art of home décor, opening with my favorite statement: "Decorating a room is a lot like dressing a man."

My comment elicited a chorus of discrete laughs hidden behind petite hands and a lot of enthusiastic nods. It was a mixed group of trendy 20- and 30-something women with animated expressions and a few conservatively dressed women closer to my age. We nodded in polite recognition; we were members of the same club.

"In the language of decorating we refer to this as 60/30/10. Sixty percent is the suit, 30 percent is the shirt and 10 percent is the tie. In a room, 60 percent are the main walls, 30 percent the trim or an accent wall and 10 percent the accessories."

We took a trip around the huge poster of a color wheel I had taped to the flip chart. I used it to identify decorating schemes like monochromatic, complementary and analogous. As part of my presentation I gave my audience the same hints I used when I put colors together for customers.

"Mono means one. So a monochromatic color scheme uses colors of the same hue or from the same color family. You can pick a principle color and use lighter or darker tones. Everything goes together. It's easy and it's a safe bet for those less adventurous customers.

"Complementary? Think of opposites attracting one another, only these colors will last longer than most relationships."

I drew a straight line across the color wheel from red to green, then another from yellow to blue.

"You can mix and match different saturation levels, like a light pink with a medium green. What does it say? To me it says tulip. Think of all the wonderful combinations in nature if you need help."

Next I drew an arc on the color wheel connecting color families that were next to each other.

"Analogous colors are neighbors on the color wheel. Welcome to the neighborhood. Look at this lovely combination of yellow, yellow green and green."

Finally I came to my favorite scheme, just because it's so damn complicated: triadic. "Think of it as a love triangle. Who says color is boring?" To finish the lesson I drew a triangle on the color wheel at eleven, three and seven o'clock to illustrate the concept. I pulled some color chips from the display and quickly put together a few different color combinations. There were appreciative gasps.

"Easy, isn't it?"

I switched gears to selling color and helping customers find the right ones. Laura picked up with her trends and we ended with an informal session over tea. The questions were pretty standard, most relating to the material covered. Soon the audience broke off into smaller groups to compare notes.

An outgoing young woman sporting a fuchsia top, leggings and rhinestone-studded suede boots approached me. "What color scheme do you have at home?" she asked. It was an unexpected personal question. One hardly ever hears personal inquiries in Asia. Heck, it had taken Laura three years to ask me such a thing. I thought I heard a hiss from some of the older sales assistants over in the far corner.

Undeterred, she waited patiently for an answer. It wasn't a faux pas. It was the next generation expressing itself openly, in contrast with the deference and reserve shown by their parents' generation. As a North American raised in an open society and now watching a steady dose of reality television, I wasn't disturbed by the question.

I smiled mischievously. "Well, let's just say that it used to be monochromatic, lots of neutrals and taupes, until I made a decision to add one little color to my life."

"What color is that?" she asked.

I slid my foot across the floor in an elegant sweep and exposed the soles of my Christian Louboutin shoes. "Red, of course."

Part Two:
Color Blind

CHAPTER 8:
A DATE WITH DESTINY

Ain't no such thing as a Hollywood ending. —The Bag Lady

The first thing I did after graduating with my newly minted journalism degree in advertising was set up interviews with ad agencies in Manhattan. Getting the interviews was easy; getting hired was another matter entirely. In 1982 the agencies were cutting back staff and eliminating their entry-level training programs. I bounced from J Walter Thompson and Ogilvy & Mather to BBDO and McCann–Erickson: legendary Madison Avenue agencies, all; and dream jobs, if I could just get one.

"We'd love to hire you but..." were the last words I heard as one door after another closed. "Great portfolio, but . . ." Even my language skills, while desirable, weren't going to help me vault over the competition. We were all in the same boat and it was sinking along with the economy. It was one of the worst recessions in history.

"The best I can do for you," one sympathetic account supervisor said, "would be a job as a receptionist, but at what we're paying you'd have to live in New Jersey and commute."

I thanked him politely and decided I'd be better off in Cleveland. I wanted to live in New York, not New Jersey.

New York was supposed to be my stepping-stone to France. A job at a major multinational agency in New York was going to be my ticket to its Paris office. Going back to Cleveland would be taking a giant step backward. There was no guarantee I'd find a job in my major in that old tool and die town, anyway. Most of the women I knew who worked "internationally" in Cleveland were in the export department filling out paperwork and customs invoices; so much for higher education.

I chose to think of it as a temporary setback. My dream wasn't dead, merely deferred. I would build experience, perhaps with a small agency in Cleveland; I would live at home, save money and try finding a job in Paris. Forget New York, I thought. There were other roads that would lead to a job where I could speak French and travel.

I pounded the pavement looking for any job. For six months I temped at offices as either a secretary or receptionist. Finally my luck changed and I was hired at a small weekly newspaper. I was back in familiar territory, writing ad copy and selling advertising space. It was a long way from all things French, though, so I decided to compromise and take my first real adult vacation in the Canadian province of Quebec, where people speak French.

The day before I was scheduled to leave was a hectic one at the office. "Bernie, I need those tear sheets for Danner Buick this morning, please," I called out to the circulation manager.

"Rush, rush, rush, Cat. You're always in such a hurry. Whaddya got? A hot date?" He glanced at his watch. It was 8:30 a.m.

Bernie Goldblum chomped on an unlit cigar. It danced up and down between his lips when he talked. He was supposed to retire five years earlier but somehow it slipped his mind. Just like my tear sheets. Short and stocky and slightly balding on top, he always wore red suspenders. It took every ounce of discipline not to snap them.

"As a matter of fact, I do—with my orthodontist."

"Not a doctor, but okay. Is he Jewish?"

"Bernie. Uh, I'm not looking for a husband. I'm looking to get these off today!" I pointed to the wires on my teeth.

"Mazel tov shayneh maidel."

"Thank you, Bern."

"Now maybe you can have some of those bagels, fatten you up a bit." He pointed to a dish next to the coffee machine. It was piled high with fresh bagels from the deli downstairs. "A man likes a woman with some meat on her bones, even if he is an orthodontist."

Who knew there would be a double benefit with braces? Not only were my teeth straight, but I'd lost 20 pounds. As I was on the verge of becoming a new woman, I certainly wasn't about to go back to the old one. No bagels for me.

"I'll be back after lunch." I grabbed my bag and headed out the door.

After my orthodontist appointment I headed straight to the travel agency to pick up my plane ticket. I pictured the tranquil and idyllic city I would soon be flying off to. I was looking forward to a little peace and quiet after a very hectic first year in the working world. I didn't realize it at the time, but I was about to learn that I kept referring to my imagined destination as Montreal. I made no distinction between the teeming metropolis and the quaint Quebec City of my dreams. All that mattered was that I was going to a place where I could speak French.

I was so lost in my thoughts I nearly tripped over the bag lady sitting in front of the bus shelter. She was holding a sign that read "$1 for a piece of my mind."

Preoccupied, I misread it as "$1 for peace of mind." I could certainly use some peace of mind, I thought.

I fished in my wallet, pulled out a dollar and put it in the paper cup she was holding. She was right; I felt better, more at peace—that was until she stopped me as I walked past her. "Hey, girlie, yeah you, Red!"

"Excuse me?"

"You paid for some advice, I'm going to give it to you."

"Huh?" And then I reread the sign.

"Ain't no such thing as a Hollywood ending," she said with a hoarse laugh. A smoker's cough rattled her chest.

What?

As a newly minted career girl (pre-*Sex and the City*) and as someone who was just starting out on her life's journey, I did not want to hear these words. Obviously there was no Hollywood ending for her, I thought as I hurried past. I worried that whatever bad luck clung to her might attach itself to me. There had to be an exception, at least for me. The bus pulled up and I hopped on, happy to leave her behind. Just in case, though, I made the sign of the cross.

The braces off and the teeth cleaned and polished, I smiled at myself in every plate-glass store window along Detroit Avenue. I couldn't wait to show my new look to my best friend and self-proclaimed personal travel consultant, Sophia Rizzo. Her family owned the neighborhood travel agency and she was just learning the business.

Sophia had laughing brown eyes and a mop of black corkscrew curls that gave her the illusion of a girl who was always in motion, even when she was sitting still. I pushed open the door of the agency and a little bell tinkled. Four dark-haired female heads looked up from their desks.

"Ciao a Tutti," I said.

Sophia jumped up from her desk. "Oh my God, Cat, you look like a different person. You look great!"

"Thanks, Soph. It certainly took long enough."

"Boy, are you going to wow those French-Canadian guys."

"That's the furthest thing from my mind," I said, smiling slyly.

"Liar! That will cost you a couple of Hail Marys."

"Eh," I waved my hand, "I'm going to go practice my French. And maybe see about getting a job there."

"*Ma,* why would they want to hire you? They've already got a whole city of French-speaking people."

"Well, they don't have me," I said, feeling a bit bold now that my braces were off.

Sophia escorted me to her desk and pulled out an envelope. She pushed it toward me. I opened it and stared at my 21-day advance purchase supersaver ticket. Little did I know that ticket, and the string of events that came with it, would have lasting implications for the rest of my life.

"You're going to have a great time in Montreal; good restaurants, nice bars, smoky jazz and lots of after-hours clubs. Party central," Sophia said.

"What are you talking about? It's a quaint old provincial town with that beautiful Chateau overlooking the St. Lawrence. You know, it has cobblestone streets, the three stone arches. It's picturesque and quiet," I said.

"What are you talking about?" Sophia asked with a squint.

"Montreal," I said.

"That's not Montreal, that's Quebec City."

"What? Quebec City? What do you mean Quebec City?" My voice was on the verge of panic.

Sophia let out a puff of air.

"New York, New York?"

"Yes," I said, trying to follow her.

"Quebec City, Quebec." She raised her eyebrows in her best "get it?" look.

"What?" I let out a string of expletives. "So where am I going?

"Montreal!"

I could practically see the thought balloon over Sophia's head with the words in big, bold type: Idiot! And she was right. How embarrassing. Here I was, the would-be world traveler, and I couldn't even make it across the border. I should have known better, taken my time (there's that hurry thing again) and done my homework.

"Can't you change it?"

"It's a supersaver. No changes."

"Great, just great," I said.

"Hey, what's the worst that could happen?"

Where had I heard that before? But for me, this whole mix-up was an innocent and interesting mistake. Experience had taught me that this could be just another adventure in my life. I was going alone and wasn't meeting anyone, so it really didn't matter where I went. I would leave this one up to fate. To paraphrase a quote from *Casablanca*, "destiny takes a hand."

The next day I arrived in Montreal with only the name of the hotel and the brochures Sophia had given me. I had no itinerary and definitely no expectations. Luckily, Montreal is an easy city to navigate. I took the Metro to Place D'Armes and grabbed a bite of lunch in Old Montreal. With its cobblestone streets, 17th-century architecture, wrought iron lamps and tiny alcoves filled with artisans, walking in Old Montreal is like stepping back in time. I half-expected to see *trappeurs* with their Mohawk guides heading to the local trading post, horses laden with furs; somber black-clad priests hurrying to church; and haggling women at the market stalls on Place Jacques Cartier, children clinging to their homespun cotton skirts.

When I blinked against the bright May sunshine, I found myself back on the terrace sipping a glass of white wine and nibbling on a piece of quiche. Since mine was a late lunch, the terrace was nearly empty except for a table of local businessmen. The owner came out and chatted with them briefly before stopping by to see me. He was a tall, distinguished man in his 50s. He looked very French in his chef's hat and spotless apron. He spied the camera and map on my table.

"Where are you from?"

"Cleveland."

"What have you seen so far?"

"Not much, I'm afraid. I just got here and I'm still getting my bearings."

"Why don't you take the Metro and visit the Olympic Stadium?"

"Right, the 1976 Summer Olympics. Who could forget Bruce Jenner or Nadia Comaneci? That sounds good," I responded with enthusiasm. "Merci."

He circled the stop on my Metro map. I arrived at the stadium and just missed the guided tour by ten minutes. The attendant told me I'd have to wait another 50 minutes for the next tour. She suggested I take a look around the grounds in the meantime. I found myself near the soccer field watching Montreal's professional soccer team, the Manic, practicing.

Hmm, nice legs, I thought as I watched them run back and forth across the field. Then I noticed him, a fellow spectator. He was a tall, blond man wearing Wayfarers. His hair was sun streaked, unusual for that time of year, and he wore the latest designer label. Perhaps he was also visiting; he looked like one of those California beach boys.

I was sure he was American: a Princeton haircut, square jaw and wide shoulders that tapered to a small waist. I bet his eyes are blue, I thought. Ooh la la! I would impress him with my French and have a little fun at the same time. I stopped and asked him for directions.

"Excusez-moi, est-ce que vous parlez français?" I asked.

"Mais bien sûr. Je parle français."

Shit, he's from here, I thought. I lost my bravado and quickly switched to English. "You're from Montreal?"

"I'm szorry but ah don't speak Inglish. Mais vous parlez français?"

"Yes, I do, but I need practice. Je dois pratiquer. Vous parlez pas anglais?"

"Only a lee-til bit. Et vous, vous êtes française? Parce que vous n'êtes pas Québécoise."

I must have looked puzzled because until this point I thought people from France and Quebec all spoke the same French. The good-looking stranger quickly brought me up to speed on the subtle differences between the languages and the accents. It's the equivalent of English spoken by a Brit versus an American. It was the beginning of my linguistic and cultural education. "Vous n'avez-pas un accent québécois. D'où venez-vous?" he asked.

"Des États-Unis," I answered.

"Et vous parlez français?!" He was amazed.

Oui. Lots of us do, I thought. But he was too cute for me to be *that* insulted.

"Je suis ravi," he said, as he extended his hand and introduced himself. "Gabriel de Villiers."

"Catherine O'Malley."

We shook hands. He pushed the Ray-Bans to the top of his head. I noticed his eyes were light brown, the color of milk chocolate.

We talked for five hours. Gabriel was intrigued by my stories, how I'd come to learn French and how I'd broken my ankle. He called it my "lucky accident" too. If it hadn't happened, we wouldn't have been able to exchange more than a few words. Ironically it would be the longest talk we would have in 20 years of marriage.

We commuted between cities for the next two years, one weekend a month, filling it with lots of sex and candlelight dinners; then the airfare went up and we got married.

I don't recall Gabriel ever proposing to me. It was as if we arrived at the same conclusion jointly. "We should get married," I said during one weekend rendezvous, and he agreed. Marriage, it seemed, was the next logical step. Gabriel was my first real serious relationship, so I had nothing to compare it to. I figured all relationships were like ours.

Still, it felt a bit off. We were so different; he was a carpenter and a draftsman by trade. I had a college degree and a career. We were, in the words of George Bernard Shaw, a misalliance. My mother saw it too.

"But you barely know this boy," she said.

"Well, how else am I going to get to know him? Isn't that what marriage is about?" I turned the argument back on her. "It's a good decision. I've made up my mind."

The truth was that with every passing day and every wedding expense—the hall, the cake, the dress, the booze—I was less sure I wanted to do this. Pride and embarrassment kept me from talking about my feelings to any one. I had never asked for advice and I wasn't about to start now.

Every week Gabriel sent money toward our wedding. He was getting excited about the event and the honeymoon in Paris. He had never traveled to Europe before; the farthest he had ever traveled was Cleveland.

My dad looked at the guest list. "Is this a wedding or a coronation?" he asked.

"Those are mostly your relatives," my mother countered.

"Two hundred and fifty of our closest friends and family," he said.

"And don't forget the 12 French Canadians," I said.

"Who don't speak English," my grandmother said.

"That's okay Gram, you can speak to them in Italian," I said.

One month before the wedding Gabriel came to the city for his tux fitting. We sat in the car in the parking lot of the Great Northern Mall, and I couldn't take it any more, I had to tell him I didn't want to get married. I would pay back everything, but this wasn't going to work. We weren't going to work.

I cleared my throat. "I . . ." and that was the end of that conversation. I burst into uncontrollable sobs.

"What's wrong?" he asked in French. He still didn't speak much English.

I couldn't tell him. I couldn't get the words out. I was afraid I'd waited too long. Suddenly a cloud burst overhead and rain pelted the car. He pulled me into his lap and held me. And the more he held me, the harder I cried. I couldn't do it. I couldn't tell him.

"Nerves," I finally said.

When the big day arrived I stood with my very proud father at the top of the aisle. The organist played the "Triumphal March" from Aida. The irony of it all. It was if I had won some prize in the marriage lottery. Ugly duckling turned swan weds handsome French–Canadian husband, and they lived. . .

As I walked down the aisle on the arm of my father, I wondered what would happen if I called it off right then. We could always have a big party. The French Canadians might be put out at having come all this way for a party rather than a wedding, but most of the guests were mine anyway. Could I turn and flee like Katharine Ross in the wedding scene from *The Graduate*? I knew, somewhere deep down inside, my parents would support me.

As I looked up at Gabriel standing there, I could see tears in his eyes. Oh God, I thought, I have to go through with this. I did love him; I just wasn't sure I liked him all that much. I didn't really know him, but perhaps in time, after living together in Montreal, I would feel differently.

CHAPTER 9:
MA VIE EN ROSE (ALMOST)

Love me less and understand me more. —Cat

During the first two years of our married life, I did feel differently. Everything was new, everything a discovery. Getting to know Gabriel, getting to know my new city, a French city, finding a job, socializing with in-laws: I was so busy adjusting I barely had time to question my decision. I used my French every day, although I tried to balance it with enough English so Gabriel would also benefit.

Gabriel worked in the building industry drafting designs for prefab homes. It was all just variations on the same theme and he tended to remain apart from his co-workers. There were very few stories to share. I had landed a job in a multinational advertising agency and was working on the aviation portfolio: corporate jets and flight simulators. It was a technical and sometimes glamorous account. The agency itself had a diverse client roster and I had a team of creative colleagues. I always had a story to tell and loved to talk about my work.

"The cost of this plane is $13 million, and that's 'green' with nothing in it; no seats, no toilet, nothing," I said with enthusiasm one night over dinner. "Finishing can cost up to $5 million. They say that one executive's plane looks like an antique English tea room on the inside."

"Imagine," Gabriel said.

"How was your day?"

"Not as exciting as yours."

And so it went for a few more years. Ever the optimist, I thought I would encourage his outside interests. He was a pretty good artist and once took photography classes. Every once in a while I would bring up the idea of him taking a course at the local vocational school. Life was too short to fill it with work, television and the few activities we shared, like exploring local landmarks on weekends.

"There's a small business seminar at the *polyvalent* on Tuesdays," I said.

"I'm not interested," he said.

"But you've always said you might like to start your own business someday. You could take a course on Tuesdays and I could certainly find something to do."

I was starving for a girls' night out. Five years into our marriage and I still had no social network outside of work. My life revolved around Gabriel and our weekend activities, like apple picking in Mont-Laurier, attending the annual boat show, doing small home renovation projects or shopping for camera equipment.

We had recently moved to the suburbs to be closer to Gabriel's work, so we were spending less and less of our free time in Montreal on the weekends. My commute home was long and tedious because we lived so far from the city. If I worked late or socialized with friends from work, I didn't get home until late. Gabriel, who spent most of his time alone at the office, couldn't wait for me to return home. On one hand it was nice that he missed my company, but after a while it got to be too much.

If I did go out with colleagues on occasion, or for dinner with a client, he would pout for days. It was as though I'd offended him somehow by leaving him alone. Try as I might, I couldn't get him to understand my need to have some space and time for myself, the same time and space I would gladly give him.

Eventually I dialed down my social self and became more and more anxious and depressed as the years passed, only I didn't realize it. I ignored the little voice of doubt inside my head, the voice that kept asking, "Is this what you want for the rest of your life?"

Instead I did what many women in my situation do: I put on my game face and did what I had to do. No one was the wiser. I was the envy of friends and family.

Gabriel and I rarely touched on the subject of children. As the oldest in my family, I was used to having lots of children around; as an only child, he wasn't used to any. Gabriel said he didn't want kids, and for the moment I was relieved. I didn't want them either, at least not right away. Growing up, all I'd ever wanted was a room of my own, and now that I had one—even though I had to share it with him—I didn't want to give it up. I figured he'd come around when we were ready. Well, it turned out that neither one of us was ever ready—Gabriel because he didn't want to have children, and I because I didn't want to have his.

We got a dog instead. Actually we got a series of dogs. Owning purebred dogs was one of his three main hobbies, the other two being photography and sailboats.

The first dog, a Basset Hound named Pif, howled every night and kept the neighbors awake. He was a hunting dog who required lots of exercise, which we apartment dwellers couldn't give. We gave poor Pif to acquaintances who lived in the country.

After we moved into our house in Brossard, Gabriel found a Great Dane, Hercules, in the classified section of the local newspaper. It wasn't the dog's fault that he acted out; he was left alone all day. Gabriel of all people should have known, but he failed to recognize the similarities in Hercules and himself.

Hercules tore up the entire house within the first week. He started with our finished basement and ended with our brand new kitchen cupboards. Gabriel regretfully called the original owners, who accepted Hercules back but who kept the $750 we'd paid. It cost us another $750 to repair the damages.

We purchased, and trained, our last dog, a black Lab called Licorice, as a puppy. Labs are happiest around water. All three of us counted the days until we could take the boat out of dry dock. Until then Licorice had the run of our backyard. Unfortunately, in his exuberance, he snapped his chain. We found him playing in traffic on a busy cross street. I couldn't live with the prospect of that dog being hit by a car, so I put my foot down. Either Gabriel had to build a run or we had to sell the dog.

I wouldn't call Gabriel cheap. I would say he was fiscally conservative; he saw no need for a run when a heavier chain and a taller post would suffice. I bowed to the inevitable. We tried another chain, which didn't work, and Gabriel gave up Licorice as well. I was beginning to see why having children with him wouldn't be a good idea.

Gabriel was also hard to please.

"Merry Christmas," I said one year, handing him a small box.

He opened it and pulled out a pair of fingerless gloves and some camera lens filters. He looked at the gloves first. "Thanks, Cat," he said. "They're not exactly the right ones but I can take them back and exchange them if you still have the receipt."

He held up one of the lens filters and examined it. "I wanted the tobacco one, not the amber," he said, a note of disappointment creeping into his voice.

I was disappointed too; I'd made notes throughout the year and thought I'd purchased the right things. "They should have a registry at the camera shop. It would make things so much easier," I muttered.

"Here," he said, handing me an envelope, "it's a gift card for Ogilvy's. It's for $100. You spent about that amount on all this, right?"

Yes, I thought. At least I could buy that designer scarf I've mentioned casually only about 50 times over the past three months. I thanked him and tried not to feel sad about the fact that he just didn't get it, or me, even after seven years of marriage. Still, I consoled myself with the fact that had I told him exactly what I wanted, I wouldn't have been surprised and the net result would have been the same.

If Christmas was a low-key affair, then New Year's barely registered on our social meter. Gabriel was not the party type. Over a quiet dinner a few days into one new year, he asked in an alarmed voice, "What, you're changing jobs again?"

"New year, new job," I said.

"But you're always changing jobs."

"I need a new challenge and a change of scenery. I've learned everything I can from this last job; it's time for something new."

The truth was, in the past seven years I'd changed jobs four times; I worked at an ad agency and a PR agency, as an advertising director for a start-up company that went bust, and now was in a high-level position at Brands-R-Us—a big corporation.

"You're never happy," he said.

"Of course I'm happy. It's just sometimes I think I can do better."

He was right, though. I was unhappy, but it wasn't with the job. I wished I could tell him I was unhappy with our dull life and that I thought

I could do better without him. I wished I could tell him that I wanted heat, passion, excitement. I wanted to live out of a suitcase—my red suitcase, to be exact. And that's why I was taking this new job. It required me to travel.

"But you were already doing so well at the ad agency," he persisted. "They gave you a promotion and then you left."

I was the principal breadwinner and could understand Gabriel's nervousness. It was my job that funded our lifestyle: suburban house, a sailboat, his motorcycle, his camera equipment, a series of poor pooches and a nice wardrobe for me.

"You know, Cat? Someday someone is going to look at your job history and think you're not dependable, and you won't be able to get another job."

"Is that what you think? That I'm not dependable?"

"I'm not saying that. I think employers will say that."

"And if you ever lose your job," I countered, "I think employers will say you have limited experience. And then what would you do? You don't know how to do anything else."

"Don't change the subject. Why do you take this job? You'll never be home."

"It's a good opportunity for me. It's a highly visible position within the company, and I think adding travel to my resume will be good for me. Just think of all those frequent-flyer miles. We'll be able to travel for fun and it won't cost us anything. The miles will pay for the planes and the hotels."

He stopped to consider the added benefit of free travel, but he wanted to have the last word. "I don't know why you bother. You're only going to change jobs again next year. This can't be good for your retirement account."

"Gabriel, please, for once, love me less and understand me more."

It was true that travel was good for our marriage. It gave me the freedom I craved and it introduced Gabriel to a brand new world beyond our suburban Montreal life. I took him on business trips with me whenever I could. Sometimes he even attended functions that included spouses. When he did, he always made an effort. He was unpretentious and funny, and it helped that he was handsome and had a charming French accent. Gradually, over time, almost imperceptibly, he learned to speak English.

Women were drawn to him and my male colleagues were happy they didn't have to entertain their wives. I was proud of him. Why, God, I prayed, couldn't it always be this way?

The added benefit to my extensive travel schedule was that we were able to enjoy some wonderful vacations at very little cost. We went to Hawaii twice, Western Canada, Chicago, New York and San Francisco, and even did the California State Route 1 drive down to L.A. An avid photographer, Gabriel looked forward to these vacations. Unfortunately, he reverted to his solitary lifestyle as soon as we were back home.

"These photos are beautiful," I said one day, sifting through some 11-by-14-inch prints. "I'm sure you could sell these. Maybe you should open your own gallery."

"No, I wouldn't want to do that. That would make it work, and I do this for fun."

"I understand."

"Where are you going now?" he asked.

"I'll be in Atlanta this week."

"Call me when you get to the hotel."

I called home every night at suppertime and we talked for a few minutes. Later in the week our conversation took a different turn.

"Cat, the company asked me if I'd take a new position in customer service. We're expanding into Ontario, and since my English has improved they asked me to start a department."

"Wow, that's really great. It's a great compliment to you that they recognize your ability."

Gabriel would have been content to stay in the same drafting position until he retired. "I don't think I want to do it," he said.

My heart sank. This new position would force him into a more public role, dealing with people on a regular basis. And who knows? He might make some friends.

My marriage fantasy didn't involve a house and a white picket fence. It was a Bailey's commercial. It involved several happy couples in their 30s, socializing over dinner, clinking glasses, smiling, laughing and enjoying each other's company. Here was another opportunity for him, for us, to have that. I needed to be careful, though. If I showed too much enthusiasm he definitely wouldn't take the job.

"I think you should do whatever makes you feel comfortable. If you're uncomfortable and don't want to take the job, you shouldn't force yourself."

Those words stuck in my throat but I knew if I encouraged him he would decline the offer and the company would find someone else. I thought I would try a little reverse psychology for a change. Instead of being an enthusiastic supporter I pretended I couldn't care less. I was shocked and amazed the following day when he announced during our nightly phone call that he would take the job.

"Are you sure?" I asked, trying not to sound too excited. "I mean, life is too short to force yourself to do something you don't like."

He insisted he was fine with the new position. I couldn't believe it.

"Are they going to give you a raise?"

"I didn't ask about that," he said. "Isn't it enough they offered me the job?"

No, it isn't. You should have asked, I thought, but I kept my opinion to myself.

That was our problem. It was all about control. I would gladly surrender control if I thought for one minute he was capable of taking care of us. If I could trust him with some of the daily responsibilities for the house, the retirement funds, the bills and other day-to-day chores. But he had just demonstrated again that if I let go we would flounder listlessly through our lives together. On the other hand, Gabriel lived his life untouched by stress. Perhaps it's a good thing not to have two stressed-out people in a marriage.

Sometimes I longed for another man, a true partner with whom I could share all of the bliss and some of the burdens of a life lived jointly. I'd managed on my own from a very young age with little or no outside help, so I decided to continue on my own, putting one foot in front of the other. The bad news was Gabriel didn't participate in our marriage; the good news was he didn't interfere. Now he was voluntarily making a move out of his comfort zone. Perhaps it was a sign of good things to come.

I was hopeful, but hope keeps gamblers going back to the casino; it keeps fans rooting for underdog teams, year after year; and it keeps women imprisoned in impossible relationships.

CHAPTER 10:
BLEEDING HEARTS

Tu est un vrai sans cœur. (You're heartless.) —Gabriel

I glanced quickly in the rear-view mirror at the receding Montreal skyline. The windows of the brightly lit skyscrapers sparkled like sequins against a blue-black sky. As I crossed the Champlain Bridge, heading home, I felt like a cheating spouse leaving her lover. If I was in love with anything, it was this city. Yet I had to admire my lover from afar. My life was securely anchored in a sleepy suburb out of reach and out of sight of the life I had once pictured.

Just as I stole another glance backward, the sound of a horn brought me back to reality. I was drifting into the neighboring lane. The bridge was icy and if I wasn't careful I'd end up in the St. Lawrence River. The prospect of a watery end, for one scary second, didn't disturb me at all. I dreaded the scene I knew was waiting for me at home.

In my mind, my life played out like some bad B movie that went straight from release to DVD. For years I tried to convince myself and everyone else that Gabriel and I lived the quintessential Hollywood ending. I loved telling the story of how we'd met. I loved hearing people say, "Wow, just like in the movies." I spoke with feigned enthusiasm of how fate had brought us together. Everyone just assumed we would live happily ever after. The reality was much, much different. We did not enjoy romantic dinners out, plays, concerts, or gallery openings together. These weren't his *thing*. So I pretended they didn't matter to me.

How was I to know that after two years of distance dating and 24 perfect weekends that included all of these things, that our relationship was merely an illusion? We were two people on their best behavior, trying to please one another. We'd even adopted some of each other's interests, but that was also short-lived. After a few years of marriage we reverted back to our prenuptial selves. Individually we were fascinating, on paper we were perfect, but together we were a misalliance. I barely knew him and he didn't understand me.

I'm not blameless in any of this. It's always easier for me to point the finger at someone else than admit I'd made the mistake. I remembered a quote from economics class that described our marriage perfectly. "Given the choice between changing one's mind and proving there's no need to do so, most people get busy on the proof." I guess it's the same thing for love. Three years became five, which quickly became seven, and now I had spent the last ten years trying to prove I had made the right choice.

Gabriel went from being my husband to being my project. Like most women my age, I saw him as a fixer upper, a work in progress. The reality was more like take it or leave it. The model was not upgradeable. He was neither a marketing campaign nor a piece of software.

I cranked up the defrost setting. My unconscious sighs had fogged up the windshield.

The evening I'd just spent in the city had been wonderful. It was the company's national sales meeting and the entire team was in Montreal to work and play. Over dinner I had flitted from table to table, talking, flirting and joking with colleagues. It happened to be my birthday, so there had been surprise birthday cake and champagne. When my colleagues sang "Happy Birthday," I'd had to hold my tears in check. Gabriel and I really didn't celebrate birthdays all that much; in fact, most holidays came and went with little or no fanfare. If one of us wanted or needed anything we usually got it for ourselves.

I had worked very hard at Brands-R-Us and had been promoted to marketing and communications director in record time. The large corner office came with a hefty $55 million advertising budget and a staff of three. I had also acquired a personal assistant, Annie Lachance, who was trained as a professional assistant and secretary. At 26 she was as telepathic as she was efficient. Her talent for anticipating my needs and reading my mind was amazing.

Annie kept my schedule, set up my meetings, helped with marketing research and kept me focused, especially on those days my mind was preoccupied with personal problems. No one but Annie knew I was balancing on the edge of a knife. Annie made sure it didn't show professionally and she tried to act as a buffer personally. She also didn't pull punches. She was more direct than diplomatic, and that was okay. I needed that.

Earlier that day Annie had thrust a garment bag into my arms. "Here. Wear this."

"What is it?"

"A cocktail dress. Monique sent it over from Ogilvy's. You'll need it for tonight."

I glanced down at my sensible Jones of New York suit. "But this will work just fine."

Ten years my junior, Annie was dressed in a white blouse, plaid mini-skirt, black tights and high-heeled suede boots. She looked like she belonged in a poster for a trendy Montreal boutique like Le Château or Mexx. She looked me over and said, "It's a bit, hmmm, what's the English word? Ah yes, 'dowdy.'"

"Dowdy?" My voice rose. "Do you think I look dowdy?"

"Dowdy and drab."

"What do you really think, Annie?" I asked.

After dinner the entire group had gone dancing at a local club. We'd danced the Lambada, a sexy and provocative dance. I hadn't danced a single step since my wedding ten years earlier, but tonight I hadn't sat down once. I'd wanted to stay as long as I could but I knew Gabriel would be up waiting for me. He wasn't happy when I called to say I'd be leaving at midnight instead of ten o'clock as originally planned. Tonight the silence on the end of the line had said it all, but I didn't care.

As I entered our house, I hoped he had fallen asleep. I slipped my heels off and tiptoed into the hallway, trying not to wake him. But there he was, waiting for me. His arms were crossed and he had a pained look on his face. It said, how dare I have a good time without him?

"Tu es un vrai sans cœur," he bleated.

I was expecting a comment on my lateness, not a charge that I was heartless. Where did that come from? I wondered.

My first instinct was to soothe and apologize, and then I remembered that I hadn't done anything wrong. I brushed past him as if nothing had happened.

"What? What did I do?"

His strategy changed and he became angry. "Why," he asked, pointing his finger at my chest, "are you still on the pill when we're not having sex anymore? Who are you sleeping with, Cat? Someone from the office?"

I stepped backward and covered my heart with my hand. Denial would be useless here. He wouldn't believe me anyway. I went for a scientific explanation instead. Sometimes it was just too easy and I took comfort in that fact.

"I'm perimenopausal and the doctor said I should be on the pill."

He didn't know how to respond to that, and I suppressed a smile. I was nowhere near menopause, peri or otherwise, but he couldn't refute the explanation.

Thwarted, he stomped out of the room. "You think you're so smart. That you have an answer to everything," he yelled over his shoulder.

I surveyed my surroundings and muttered to myself, "I must not be that smart. I'm still here."

As I brushed my teeth I fantasized about packing a bag and walking out the front door. If tonight's display of recrimination was any indication of what would happen, I decided it was best to do nothing. I didn't know how he'd handle my leaving and I had nowhere to go.

I didn't want the end of our marriage to be my fault, but somebody had to take the decision and it wouldn't be Gabriel, no matter how bad things got. Why would he give up the house, car, sailboat, motorcycle—in short, his lifestyle—because his wife was unhappy? That was my issue, not his. He was perfectly content.

I glanced around the house. Gabriel would never give this up, I thought. And that thought led to the next. What if I said I wanted to go home to Cleveland and start over? What if I said I wanted a fresh start? He'd never go for it, not in a million years. It was brilliant. Rather than argue, I would implement a change so drastic it was bound to force a wedge between us. I would resign from Brands-R-Us in the morning and return to Cleveland with or without him. If he didn't choose to come, well, that was his decision, his fault. I would be free.

CHAPTER 11:
A FRESH START

And now it's up to me. —Cat

I really didn't think he would do it. I didn't even consider the possibility he would leave the creature comforts of Montreal suburbia to start over in Cleveland. I thought he'd back down from my ultimatum, that it would force a split. We could blame our divorce on the move, on irreconcilable geographical differences. No harm, no foul as they say in basketball.

But he did. He gave up everything and followed me. The two of us now found ourselves in a new city and unemployed. I had taken this decision on the fly and our house had sold more quickly than we thought it would; therefore, we weren't quite as prepared as I would have liked for a major move and a change of country. I made a decision and I went with it. Now we were in our mid-30s and living in my parents' basement along with most of our furniture. The stress was unbelievable.

I put on my game face for my parents, but somehow they weren't buying the charade. The one and only person I could talk to, my beloved grandmother, had died several years before. Her last words to me were "I love you Catherine," whispered weakly over a phone line as if it were just another day, and not her last.

I now sat in the bedroom we'd once shared, and cried. She was gone but I could still feel her presence. I put the little red suitcase under her twin bed. "And now it's up to me," I whispered.

The next day I received a call from Canada. Jonathan Trask and I had worked together on a project for Brands-R-Us. Jon was a bright young entrepreneur in the process of aggressively growing his family business internationally. I had purchased some software from his company and we had instantly hit it off and stayed in touch. We had both come of age in the

1970s. We shared the same historical and cultural context as well as the same taste in music. We also shared a common experience: a Catholic high school education as kids with the same rebellious streak.

"Hey, Cat, rumor has it you moved back to the US. Do you have a job lined up yet?"

"Not yet, I just started interviewing. Why?"

"Because I'd like to hire you."

"To do what?"

"Sell for me."

"Software?"

"No, that's only a small part of our business. We produce color-merchandising tools for the paint industry. You're within 20 minutes of the two leading national brands. I'm two plane rides away from those same companies."

"What kinds of tools? You mean those little paint chips?"

"Yes, and fan decks and architect kits. It's everything a paint company needs to show colors to consumers, designers and architects."

"I thought paint companies did that."

"Nope, we do. It's not their core business, it's ours."

"Paint chips," I repeated.

"It's more than that. We're marketers of our customers' products; you're selling value-added services like strategy and marketing, trends and research, anything to set us apart from the competition."

I hadn't sold anything in years. I wasn't sure I possessed the technical savvy to sell specialized merchandising tools. I did know a thing or two about printing from my days at the newspaper and ad agency, but was it enough?

Jon continued, "You could work from home, although there is some travel involved."

"Really."

"Yes. I was thinking of adding Montreal to your sales territory. You speak the language. It would be a great way to stay in touch with friends. You could even keep your favorite hairdresser."

I smiled at how well he knew me. "Hey, a girl's gotta do what a girl's gotta do; didn't you once tell me that?" he asked.

"Yes, just as I was signing the contract for that innovative decorating software program you sold me," I replied.

"And . . ."

"And it turned out to be a good investment."

"So here we are again," he said.

"Well, since you put it that way, maybe I'll think about it."

"I want you to think about one more thing. This travel I was talking about is more than Montreal. Montreal will be your hub for bigger things."

"Do you want me to look after the rest of Canada as well?"

"No. Europe."

"I'll take it!"

Everything was settled within a month's time. We moved out of the basement and into a brand new townhouse. Gabriel found work.

"How did it go at Elite Home Builders, did you get the job?"

"I didn't go. I got sidetracked and stopped at Car Corp Insurance. They were looking for a call center manager."

"What did you say when they asked if you have any experience?"

"I own a house, a boat and a motorcycle. I know a little something about insurance."

"And they hired you just like that?"

"Just like that," he said, then added, "Obviously my limited experience was not an issue. They hired me anyway."

"Touché."

He was finally able to prove a point. His meaning was clear; his wife didn't have all the answers. Spending ten years in the same job didn't limit his ability to move to a new industry after all. It didn't pay as much as a drafting position, but that wasn't the point. He was right and I was wrong in this respect.

I couldn't care less. I was happy if he was happy, and it would be interesting to see how he liked this new job since it involved dealing with a much broader public. Now maybe we'd have something to talk about, stories to trade and experiences to share. It would be good training for life in Cleveland, living among my large, noisy and loving family.

There is just no way to be unsociable in a family as big as mine. It's who we are. We attend wakes with the same enthusiasm as weddings. Both are opportunities to come together and celebrate life. But Gabriel didn't really want to put up with friends and relatives. He preferred the company of strangers to them. His being new on the job gave him a legitimate excuse to avoid many family functions, and my friends and family got used to my showing up solo.

If only he took the time to get to know my family, I thought. But he wasn't interested. In his free time he took his camera to local parks, rode his motorcycle or shopped on-line for a new dog. He turned down tickets to concerts, plays and sporting events. He was content to stay home.

Uncle Frank, a retired cop, had another theory: "Cat's knocked him off for the insurance money and he's buried in the backyard. That's why we never see him."

Comfortably ensconced in our suburban home, we fell into a predictable pattern of *à chacun ses goûts*—to each his own—over the next eight years. We were free to pursue our own interests as long as we didn't interfere with each other's personal activities. We became roommates who split expenses. When Gabriel joined me on business trips to London, Paris or Rome, he no longer escorted me to those client dinners where spouses were invited. On non-business trips we traveled together but went our separate ways upon arrival.

While on vacation in Buenos Aires, I decided to give it, give us, another shot. We attended a professional tango show, which was, in a word, magic. We were both spellbound by the music and the movement. Gabriel spent the next two days around Caminito Avenue in La Boca District, searching for street dancers who performed tango. He got some amazing photographs. The bonus was that I was able to convince him to take tango lessons. Maybe, I thought, if we could dance together, it would be our way of communicating as a couple. Dancing would be the one thing we could enjoy together.

After only a few lessons, I was amazed at how adept he was at tango. I was so happy as he held me in his arms and led me around the *milonga*. I was happy to have him lead. At last, I thought, we have found something we can take back with us, something we can enjoy together in Cleveland. Once we returned home I got busy looking for dance schools and venues that offered tango. I finally found the right place for us and excitedly placed the brochure on the dinner table.

"Look, we can dance tango right here in Cleveland."

"I don't want to dance tango."

"But I thought you liked it."

"In Argentina."

"It doesn't have to be tango if you want to try something else like salsa or cha-cha. I'm open. Whatever you want."

"I only danced because you asked me to."

"I see. And if I asked you again?"

"No, I don't think so. It would be a waste of time and money for me."

I knew I had passed the point of no return when my disappointment was replaced by resignation. How fitting, I thought, that our last dance together was a tango in Buenos Aires.

We were divorced in all but name, but the mere mention of divorce or of splitting assets or, worse, of the loss of frequent-flyer miles elicited a hue and cry so loud and long that it wasn't worth it. I couldn't bear listening to him complain about how selfish I was. And so I carried on, not out of loyalty, not out of commitment, and not out of the stubborn belief that I could make anything work. I carried on out of habit.

CHAPTER 12:
UNFINISHED BUSINESS

Your mother and I never did like him. —Dad

A lightly accented voice interrupted my reverie. "Ladies and gentlemen, we're about to land in Montreal. Please ensure that all electronic portable devices have been switched off, all tray tables are closed and locked and all seats are in their upright position."

Was it only just 12 hours ago that I was having dinner in Paris with Christian at Le Chien Qui Fume in Les Halles? It felt like a lifetime ago, and perhaps it was. Instead of watching the latest box-office hit on the tiny video screen, I had watched a movie of my own making. I had seen my life pass before me as if a dream. I remembered the question I had asked myself the day before: How did I ever get here? Now I knew.

I was back in reality and about to land. The three weeks and seven hours of freedom were over. I felt the pressure of gravity and the G-force of the landing push me down into my seat. I was earth- and duty-bound.

Montreal has always been my hub of choice when flying internationally. It's well laid out like most big American airports but on a smaller scale. It has convenient connections to Cleveland and fewer crowds than Newark or Detroit. The only drawback was I had to clear customs twice.

I could navigate the Montreal airport with my eyes closed, and I often did. I would put myself on autopilot as I cleared first Canadian and then US customs before catching my connecting flight home to Cleveland. Every so often I thought about missing that flight and just staying in Montreal, but the thought was only fleeting.

Autopilot is a good thing, especially when I'm preoccupied as I was on this Air France flight from Paris. I thought about all of my client meetings and the follow-up assignments that went with them. Thoughts of everything I had to do—write proposals, finalize specifications, send samples, confirm orders—swirled in my head. There was also an important detail I couldn't quite nail down in my memory. Distracted, I nearly walked into the men's room on my way to my connecting flight.

"Madame! Madame! Ca va? Ca va?" I heard a voice say from somewhere far away. I blinked, then realized I was flat on my back looking up at a crowd of strange faces hovering above me. I reached instinctively for my purse. I found it at my side. My laptop bag lay nearby. I tried to raise myself on one elbow.

"What the . . ."

"No, don't get up," said a faceless voice in the crowd. "*Attends*! We'll call the *urgence*."

"What happened?" I asked, a little disoriented. "I'm fine, I think." I felt a lump starting to rise on the back of my head.

"You be walking through here. It's a bit slippery mon," a large black man with dreadlocks and a thick Jamaican accent explained excitedly, pointing his mop handle to the yellow plastic tent signs indicating the wet floor.

"And you slipped and fell," a young woman with pink hair and a pierced nostril said as she helped me sit up. She handed me a bottle of water.

"I guess I wasn't paying attention. I'm very sorry for all the trouble. I'm fine, really. Thank you," I said as I got to my feet with some help.

"But you're not hurt?" asked a young security guard with a tight-fitting grey polyester uniform.

"Only my pride. Did I at least fall gracefully?"

"Ha!" said an old man wearing a wide-brimmed black felt hat and sporting side curls. "It was like an old Chaplin film where you see him slipping on a banana peel and his legs go out from under him."

I felt my face starting to burn with embarrassment. "Nothing like making an entrance."

"It sounds like your sense of humor is still intact," said a middle-aged man in a well-cut suit and tie as he handed me my bags. "I'll walk you to your gate. You should really get checked out when you get home. And where would *that* be?"

"Where would what be?"

"Home?"

"Oh, Cleveland." I felt very tired. That was the detail I had forgotten. I wanted to stay right there, at the airport, and never leave.

Okay, okay, I mumbled to no one in particular, you don't have to hit me over the head.

My dad met me at the airport in Cleveland. "Glad to be home?" he asked as he hefted my suitcase out of the trunk. His hands trembled a bit with the strain.

I studied him out of the corner of my eye. When did his hair get so grey? While he still had his ruddy complexion and clear blue eyes, he seemed much shorter now than just a few weeks earlier. I hated to think of him aging, but that's exactly what was happening. My big, strong dad, who held my hand as he walked me to school, was becoming a shadow of his former self.

I kissed his cheek. "You betcha!" I mustered a smile. "Thanks again for coming to get me. Gabriel's schedule at the call center is crazy right now."

"Hey, don't worry about it. It's the only chance I ever get to see you without your mother monopolizing the entire conversation."

"I'm going to pretend you didn't say that," I said, smiling.

I switched on the hallway lights as my father deposited my suitcase in the hallway. "Coffee?" I offered.

"That would be nice."

I could see, as we walked into the kitchen, that the living and dining rooms were in a state of disarray. A pile of newspapers sat next to the couch. Damn, I had forgotten to cancel the paper. Why couldn't Gabe have picked up the phone and done it himself? What did he think, that I was going to read 21 days worth of newspapers when I got back?

A full laundry basket sat next to the ironing board in the middle of the living room. I couldn't tell if the clothes were clean or not. I'd have to smell them later. The dinner dishes, two place settings, were still on the dining room table.

"Company?" my father asked.

"The neighbor, probably. She pops by once in a while if her husband's away and she needs something."

I put on a pot of coffee and put the dishes in the dishwasher.

"Dad, can you pull out the cream? If Gabe cooked, there might also be some dessert left."

My father opened the refrigerator door and shook his head.

"It's empty. Doesn't your husband ever eat? There's never anything in your fridge."

I looked over my father's stooped shoulders. He was right; a lonely block of moldy cheese sat on the top shelf. I looked around the kitchen and noticed how bare it looked: an empty fruit bowl, a plastic bag with one slice of bread and an empty jar of instant coffee on the counter.

"He eats at work," I explained. "I'm sure he meant to go shopping but he probably decided to wait to see what I would like."

There it was: another excuse. I made them so often I wasn't even aware of it until my dad said under his breath, "Or maybe he was going to wait for you to do it?"

My father has been a card-carrying member of the Catholic Church from day one. A former altar boy, a baseball coach for the CYA (Catholic Youth Association) and a member of the Holy Name Society, he communicated with God on a first-name basis. He called God "Oh" and God called him "Jim." The fact that I no longer attended Mass, except for weddings and funerals, did not sit well with him, but he is not the kind of parent who tells you what to do. He and my mother liked to practice reverse psychology on their children. It was a slower process than, say, guilting us into doing something, but it eventually worked.

I wondered what he would think if I told him I was contemplating divorce from Gabriel. I, the eldest of his seven children, not to mention the eldest of 28 first cousins in our family, none of whom were divorced, was about to break the bad news to him. Mine was a lifetime of firsts, so why not me? Why not this? Why not now?

"Say listen, Dad. What would you think if I told you that I wanted to ask Gabriel for a divorce?" I held my breath, fearing the worst.

"I'd ask what took you so long."

I had already formed his imaginary response in my head, so I didn't hear his actual reply. I continued just like a good defense attorney arguing her case before a judge. "Lots of people get divorced. I don't know why you have to be so judgmental."

"Cat," he said as he held up his hands, "you should learn to listen more."

I did a quick backtrack to what he had just said.

"What?"

"Your mother and I never did like him."

"And you waited almost 20 years to tell me?"

"Hey, it's your life. You never asked our opinion so we never gave it, Miss Fourth of July." That was one of his many nicknames for me; another was Miss Independence.

"What do you mean you never liked him?"

"I almost said something a few years ago when we threw your surprise 40th birthday party."

I searched my mind and couldn't come up with anything offensive or out of the ordinary about Gabriel's behavior. "What do you mean?"

"Everyone came, all of your aunts, uncles, cousins and friends."

"Yes, and it was a blast. Thank you, Dad!"

"But he couldn't come. His excuse? Work. And it's not like we didn't give him any notice. He knew about it a month in advance. It really frosted my ass. But he managed to get off work to fly to Paris, two weeks later, on your points, when you went there on business, right?"

I'd never thought about that. That's just Gabriel. I could never count on him to show up at social events. I was the social butterfly and he was the caterpillar happy at home in his cocoon. Friends got so used to setting and removing a place for him during dinner parties that it became somewhat of a running joke. Since I was among family and friends, I never missed him. I got used to him not being there.

As the eldest, I'd lived a lifetime of compromises. Why would my marriage be different? Except Gabriel wasn't a child; he was my husband, and compromise was a two-way street. It occurred to me that my father was right. Gabriel always made the time when it came to things that were convenient or that pleased him.

"Then you're okay with it?" I couldn't quite believe it.

"All we ever wanted, your mother and I, was for you kids to be happy. Was it really that hard to tell me?" He looked hurt.

"No, it wasn't. It's just that in the past your bark has always been worse than your bite."

He laughed. "True."

I can't remember when I stopped talking to my father. It was probably after college, when I thought I knew everything. Suddenly I realized how much I had missed him, his advice and his experience. He was always there for me as a kid, but as an adult I had felt I needed to figure things out for myself. I could feel the tears begin to well in my eyes.

"Road trip?" he asked.

"Nah, that's okay."

My father's answers to life's most difficult problems always came to him from behind the wheel of a car. It was kind of like a confessional. I could spill my guts in an oblique fashion while looking at the scenery, with no embarrassment or hesitation. He'd pretend to concentrate on his driving while I tried to explain how I felt.

With four daughters there was always some crisis to be averted, anger managed, perspective adjusted or broken heart mended. Superman always had his cape and my father always had a clean hanky at the ready. A product of the 1950s, he never left home without three things in his back pocket: his wallet, his comb and his hanky. I never saw him use the hanky, himself; it was reserved especially for his girls, his damsels in distress.

He pulled the hanky out of his back pocket and handed it to me, just as the first tear slid down my check. What followed was a torrent of pent-up emotion. I hadn't cried like that since my grandmother died.

"Don't feel bad, honey. You don't have to feel bad about this at all. We're right behind you." My dad wrapped me in his arms.

I didn't feel bad. That's not why I was crying. I was crying from relief, and because of that, I cried all the harder.

I had finally made a decision. For years I had hoped it would be Gabriel who would ask for a divorce, to take the burden of guilt from me. But why would he when he was obliviously happy with the way things were, the way we were? Why would he ever want a divorce?

CHAPTER 13:
WE'VE GOT TO TALK

You're never happy. —Gabriel

I looked at the figures all afternoon; with no children involved, ours would be a simple divorce. Provided he didn't contest it, it would be a dissolution. Did that mean I'd be a disolvée rather than a divorcée? Hi, I'm Cat, and I'm dissolved. The absurdity of the category made me laugh, but it was really just gallows humor.

No matter what I said, no matter how I said it, I knew this was going to be bad. Gabriel would either have to be blind or in deep denial to miss the fact that we had limped along as a couple for years, with no hope for recovery. There's no good time to break bad news. I looked at my watch and realized he would be home any minute.

"I didn't know you were back today," he said, a look of surprise crossing his face when he entered the living room.

"Didn't you get the voice mail?"

"I forgot to check," he said as he tossed his coat on the back of a chair.

"You also forgot to clean up." I glanced around the room.

"Sorry, I'll help you tomorrow. How was the trip?"

"Long."

"That's a lot of frequent-flyer miles. What do you think about Hong Kong?"

"I think it's very far away. The last thing I want to do is get on another airplane." I unconsciously touched the bump on the back of my head.

"You wouldn't have to go. That is, unless you really want to. I think I could get some amazing photos over there."

"Give me a day or two to catch up and I'll see about getting you a flight."

Nervous, I busied myself unpacking my laptop case as casually as I could while trying to think of a way to broach the subject of divorce. I pulled out the piece of deep red watered silk and put it on the dining room table. Next to it I placed a fan deck. I opened it to the red section and began looking for a paint chip that would match the fabric.

"*Merci, ma belle.*" He kissed me on the top of my head, then paused. "What's this?"

"I want to paint the bedroom this color."

"That's crazy. It will ruin the value of the house."

There it was: my opening. I silently thanked my grandmother who was at that moment watching out for me.

"You mean the value of *your* house Gabriel. This has never been my house. Every time I want to try something different, you always say no." I took a deep breath before continuing. "For years I've tried, I mean we've tried, to make something out of our lives together. Yet after all this effort, we've never accomplished much as a couple."

"What do you mean we've never accomplished much?"

We, or I, I should say, had attempted this kind of discussion once or twice before, so he knew where I was going with it. "I want a divorce, Gabriel. This time I mean it." I pointed to a small bag I had packed earlier in the day. The spare bedroom at my parents' house was ready.

"*Mon Dieu,* what's wrong this time Cat? Tell me, did they lose your luggage or something? Is that why you're in such a bad *humeur*—"

"Mood," I absentmindedly corrected him. "And no, I'm not in a bad mood."

"Look at this, look at what we've got here." He gesticulated wildly at our beautifully appointed house. "I don't understand. You're free to do whatever you want. You can come and go as you please. We never argue, except for these silly things. It's like we're not even married."

"But that's exactly my point! We're not married, not really. Our lives run in parallel. And I want to be married."

He looked confused. "You know what's wrong with you?"

I bit my tongue because a whole list of wrongs was about to crest the mental dam that held back years of suppressed wants, needs and desires. I didn't want to prolong the argument. I didn't want to lose courage and retreat to the comfortable, to habit, to peace at any price.

"You're never happy!" he shouted.

"You'll never be able to understand this, but no, I am not! I have tried to explain this to you and you've always glossed over things unless they were important to you. So you're right. I agree. You win. I'm unhappy, and I'm leaving."

I picked up my suitcase, grabbed my car keys and left a stunned Gabriel surrounded by stacks of newspapers, a table full of dirty dishes, a basket of laundry and an empty refrigerator. My heart was beating hard in my chest and my breath came in shallow gasps. My hand shook as I tried to insert the key into the ignition. It was the same adrenaline rush I had once experienced after narrowly avoiding a two-car collision. I drove the two miles to my parents' house very carefully.

My parents had given up our old home in the city and had moved to the suburbs years ago. I had lived in the new house for only a few years before getting married and moving out. That night I returned to a bedroom that was as strange as it was familiar. I had shared the room with my grandmother the year before I got married nearly 20 years earlier.

Despite the familiar surroundings and the silent support of my parents, sleep eluded me that night. Anxieties, not for me but for Gabriel, invaded my exhausted brain. What if he did something rash? How would he handle the finances? Who would pay the bills and the taxes, negotiate the car and house insurance? Who would fight with the city over the commercial property being built across the street? It certainly wouldn't be Gabriel.

I felt guilty. He was a stranger in a strange country, far from his home and family. He had given up everything just so I could be close to mine. Never mind the fact he phoned his family only on major holidays and birthdays, or that he would rather fly 14 hours to Hong Kong than one hour to Montreal. He was who he was, and there was no changing him.

Try as I might, I knew there was no changing myself either. If he didn't like his life here, he was free to go. We were both free to go anywhere that made us happy. I couldn't worry about him anymore. It was time to worry about myself. I wanted to get back to being me. Once I made peace with that thought I fell asleep and into a dream.

I saw myself in a church. I was nine years old and wearing a wedding dress that was too big for me. My grandmother held my left hand as we walked down the aisle and exited the church together. I gripped the little red suitcase in my other hand. As we walked I kept tripping over the long dress.

"Grandma," the little girl who was me asked, "what happens if it doesn't work out? What am I going to do?"

I had asked her the same question on my wedding day. She put both hands on my shoulders and looked me in the eye. Her answer, awake or asleep, was the same: "Eh, and so what? You tried it, it didn't work, and you getta divorce. That's life." And she would know; she had divorced my grandfather, twice.

The divorce papers signed, I returned to the house I had shared with Gabriel a month later to pack the rest of my things. Gabriel kept the house and some cash. I got my freedom. There was nothing there that I wanted. Truth be told, it was decorated more to his taste than to mine or, God forbid, ours. Good riddance to it! Some would argue he got more than his fair share of assets, but I wanted to be sure this was all he ever got. My lawyer thought it was a good strategy and we got unanimous agreement. How do you put a price on freedom?

I entered the house through the garage. Once inside, I felt like an intruder. After one month it was already foreign to me. Had I ever really lived in it? Gabriel was at work. I walked into the bedroom. I was shocked to find the bed made and the clothes folded. What, had he had the sense to hire a maid already? I was impressed. Here I'd been worried about how he was going to get along without me.

I noticed a long, dark hair on the pillow. As I'm a redhead and Gabe is blond, I wondered about it. Was there someone else? I should have been mortally offended; the ink wasn't even dry on the paperwork yet. On the other hand, this was my get-out-of-jail-guilt-free card. How bad was that? Yet I was angry. He hadn't even had the decency to wait until I moved out of the house before finding what looked like my replacement, and in record time.

I wondered whether this was the first time. Had there been others? I had mechanically made our bed every day for 20 years, oblivious, or even blind, to the possibility that he could have been unfaithful.

It didn't really matter in the end. All of the righteous indignation I could muster didn't change the fact I had asked for the divorce. This was about choice, not blame. I wasn't going to blame him and I certainly wasn't going to blame myself.

We had been emotionally divorced for years. We were roommates. What little attraction there had initially been in the bedroom had dwindled once we were married. The intense longing and desire that were once stoked by distance couldn't be recreated no matter how many self-help books I read. Nothing worked. Two years' worth of weekends hadn't given us any indication of just how incompatible we really were on so many levels. Sexual compatibility was only one of them.

I took a final look around. Everything was packed and ready; my brother would be arriving shortly with his pickup truck. There were two suitcases and a dozen boxes. Twenty years of my life didn't take up a lot of space. I pressed the control panel in the garage and the door made its familiar humming sound as it slid up the track. Neighbors had decorated their homes for the holidays, and with the snow falling softly the street looked quite pretty.

I thought about my next move just as a sleek black Ford Ranger pickup backed up the driveway. A tall, handsome man in his 40s, with dark hair and dark eyes, my brother Jimmy grabbed me and embraced me in a hug so fierce it lifted me three feet off the ground.

"*Ciao, sorella,*" he said. "Ready?" He began putting the luggage into the bed of the truck. "Good move, by the way, we—"

"Yeah, yeah, I know, you never liked him anyway."

He shrugged. "Eh, is there anyone ever good enough for my sisters? You should have married a nice Dago plumber from the neighborhood, or a good Mick cop, like Uncle Frank."

"Next time."

"I'll believe that when I see it. Always going for the imported stuff." He nodded in the direction of my Honda Accord. "What's a matter with the domestic variety?" He beamed at his monster-sized truck. "At least make sure the next one speaks English or a language we understand, okay?"

"*Ma.*" I took a friendly swat at his head, and he ducked.

"Got everything?"

"Yeah, I think so," I said as I rummaged in my purse for car keys. I was just about to key in the alarm code when I saw it in the corner of the garage, half-hidden behind a bag of charcoal briquettes and a pile of window screens. There it sat, quietly waiting: the little red suitcase.

DESTINATION: CHICAGO

"Quit pacing. You're making me nervous," Lennie said as she expertly thumbed her BlackBerry.

Lennie Glassman didn't look the least bit nervous. She looked neat, crisp and cool in her navy Ralph Lauren blazer, white turtleneck and camel-colored pants. Her straight, precision-cut blond hair fell into her eyes. As marketing director for America's best-known paint brand, Lennie had just closed a significant sales deal with a large home improvement retailer. Her corporate star was rising and she was counting on us to support her by providing an endless supply of color chips, which meant we had to have all of the colors available all of the time for all 2,000 stores.

It was a no-color-missing policy. Our factory went into overtime 24/7 gearing up to meet the demand. My job was to convince both Lennie and the retailer's marketing and procurement teams that we'd done our homework, analyzed the data and looked after all of the details. We wouldn't let them down.

Lennie's job was to facilitate our introduction. Her endorsement of our company carried a lot of weight with the giant retailer and within her own firm. Her job was to keep the discussion on track. "I like these kinds of presentations," she told me on the plane ride down. "It's a lot more fun when you get to watch."

The retailer's corporate office was built to impress. It was nestled in a business campus surrounded by mature trees. The landscape design, which included a reflecting pool, set off the 1950s-style modernist architecture of the buildings. I was relieved to see we were in one of the smaller conference rooms. It was located on the outside of the building's perimeter and benefited from the natural light coming in from four windows. The furniture was functional and intentionally not suited for long meetings.

I set a copy of the inventory management strategy in front of six chairs. "Twenty-five years ago," I said to Lennie, "we would have been doing this in shoulder pads and big hair."

"Twenty-five years ago we'd have been pouring the coffee," she replied, peering overtop her tortoise-shell bifocals. "Today everyone realizes the important role women play in the marketplace. We're better educated, wealthier and independent, and we pull the strings—the purse strings."

Lennie and I both came of age in the 1980s. She worked with major corporations and I worked in ad agencies. We spent the better part of a decade knocking down doors that most young women now walk through. This was more than business for both of us. It was personal.

"And we buy a lot of paint," I added.

"Speaking of paint, did you really paint your bedroom red after your divorce?"

"Not exactly red. More like Bordeaux, a deep wine red with blue undertones. It's something I always wanted to do."

I removed a plastic bag of M&Ms and a small bowl from my briefcase. "Being single is a lot like M&Ms; I have many more options now than I did a few years ago. Pick a color, any color. In my apartment there's Bordeaux in the bedroom, Serengeti in the living room, Vienna Coffee in my home office and Fragile Sky in the bathroom." I wasn't just thinking about color when I said this. Since moving back to Montreal my options seemed unlimited.

I poured the M&Ms into the bowl and placed it in the center of the oblong table. "That the new color palette?" Lennie asked.

"Sort of...they're a good example of a limited color range, which when it comes to paint is what consumers have been asking for. Your research shows that consumers are overwhelmed by too many colors. They also don't have a lot of time to choose colors. So we have to make it quick and easy for them to find what they're looking for. Your new color palette does that.

"Consumers also need some help putting colors together. So putting color schemes on the back of each chip is helpful. Our color tools support your market strategy. You're the marketing experts and we're the color experts. We want to establish a comfort level with you and the customer. We want to prove we understand what you need," I concluded.

"Okay, so far so good." Lennie stole a couple of M&Ms from the bowl.

"The M&Ms are my way of demonstrating that we're detail-oriented. You and the retailer can depend on us to deliver."

Lennie gave me an expectant look.

"Do you see anything different about those M&Ms?" I asked.

"Not really," she said.

"There aren't any brown ones."

"You're kidding." She took a good look. "Hey, you're right. How come?"

"Because of Van Halen."

"Cat, this better be good, otherwise that comfort level you just created will be history."

"The story goes that Van Halen's contract includes a clause that asks each venue to supply a bowl of M&Ms backstage without brown ones. They put this clause in their contract to see how well the venue managers have read the contract specifications. If they got the M&Ms right, there was a good chance they got the stage specifications for weight, technical and electrical requirements right too. Inadequate compliance would put their road crew in danger."

"A small but important detail," Lennie said. "Impressive. This is a detail-oriented customer and they'll appreciate your approach."

"Thanks. We have a lot of experience in that area."

While Lennie went back to her BlackBerry, I booted up my computer. I ran through my PowerPoint presentation one last time and reviewed my mental checklist to make sure I'd covered everything.

Lately I'd mastered the details of more than just candy and color. Single for over one year I'd gone on over 65 dates. After the first dozen I'd learned to pick up on the details. Noticing details early on can save a lot of time and tears down the road.

Does he look me in the eyes?

Does he arrive early and buy himself a coffee first so as not to buy me one?

Does he say he's going to call on a certain day or at a certain time and doesn't?

Does he get carried away and start planning the next three weeks, three months, three years, but ends the relationship after three days?

Does he say unflattering things about women in general?

I plugged my laptop into the projector and a colorful rendering of a paint chip display filled the flat-panel screen.

"My grandmother would say the devil is in the details," Lennie said.

"She'd be right," I said absently, thinking more about the last year than this morning's presentation.

Part Three:
True Colors

CHAPTER 14:
WONDER WOMAN RETIRES

You're like Wonder Woman. It's nice to see that you're human too. —Annie Lachance

Annie hugged me. "I can't believe you're back, it only took you how long?"

"Eleven years," I said, surveying my freshly painted apartment.

"You finally chose happiness."

"Oh, Annie." When she put it that way I felt a small pang of regret for all of that lost time. No matter. I was determined to make up for it. After all, I was only 45 years old.

Annie inclined her head toward the patio door.

"Go ahead, but you'll freeze your bum off," I said. Back in Montreal only three days, I made sure to use the right Canadian word for that part of her anatomy.

She brushed me off with a shrug as she slid into her sleek black quilted parka with gold zippers. She pulled a pack of cigarettes out of her purse and made for my snow-covered balcony.

"It's minus 25 you know. You'll catch your death of cold if the cigarettes don't kill you first," I yelled after her.

I was back "home" and living downtown—or close enough. My apartment was on the western-most edge of the city near a Metro station, a five-minute cab ride from most clubs, stores and restaurants and across the street from the bountiful Atwater Market. I looked out on the snow-covered Lachine Canal. Bare maple trees stood at attention, their spindly fingers splayed across a dirty grey sky, waiting patiently for spring.

This was my do-over. I looked around the empty apartment and exhaled a long, slow breath. I could finally breathe again. The apartment was empty except for a newly delivered queen-sized mattress and a couple of folding chairs. But it was mine to do with as I wished, to decorate as I saw fit. Prior to moving in I had found my well-worn paint swatch and given it to the maintenance manager. It was a stunning shade of red, so rich and velvety I could almost taste it. I finally had my Bordeaux bedroom. I would work on the other rooms later; the colors and décor would reflect the exotic places and cultures of my life.

The place was just two years old and kitted out in a very modern style with mahogany floors, granite countertops and chrome appliances. The overhead light fixtures were stainless steel branches with LED lights at six-inch intervals. I worried that I wouldn't be able to afford the kind of furniture that belonged in this kind of modern, über-urban environment. But at the moment, furniture was the least of my worries.

Every once in a while I'd catch myself glancing at the front door, half-expecting Gabriel to walk through it. Old habits die hard. I knew our paths would never cross again. It was a strange feeling. I couldn't believe I was on my own. Then it hit me. Oh my God, *I'm on my own.*

I sat on a folding chair and looked down at the suitcases lying open on the floor. Every day I rummaged through them searching for something to wear. The contents looked like they had gone a couple of rounds with airport security. At the very least, I thought, I should hang my clothes in the large walk-in closet, a closet that was exclusively mine. I just didn't have the energy. I would get to it; I was in no hurry. I looked around at the apartment and suddenly felt overwhelmed by its emptiness.

What to do first? I wondered. For some reason I thought I would feel more prepared. I'd dreamed of this day for years. I'd fantasized about the new furniture, new wardrobe, new independence, and new, deep, meaningful relationship I would have with him, the yet-to-be-found boyfriend. I was sure it was only a matter of time.

There wasn't a problem that Annie couldn't solve or any need she couldn't anticipate. Her efficiency was scary. When she'd worked for me at Brands-R-Us, she would present me with finished projects I didn't know I needed until she completed them. She had eventually parlayed her talents into her own concierge/event planning company and was now her own boss—and, as I now told her, the boss of me. To which she replied smoothly, "I learned from the best."

Today I was Annie's project. She planned to take me shopping at Sears for basics: linens, towels, dishes and cutlery. A blast of Arctic air hit me as she opened the patio door. She stamped the snow off her boots and onto my newspaper floor mat.

"You mean to tell me that all you have are your clothes?" she asked, rubbing her hands together. "Just these suitcases?"

"Yes."

"T'es folle."

"Not crazy, just practical."

"Cat, I wouldn't call this practical. You've got nothing. That's not practical. That's called guilt."

"No it's not! Well, maybe just a little. Okay, I hate it when you're right."

Annie laughed. "And these suitcases have been sitting here in the middle of the living room for what, a week now?"

"Noooo. Just three days."

"That's three days too many."

She pulled off her boots and shrugged out of her coat.

"What are you doing? I thought we were going shopping."

"I'm going to organize your closet first. I can't stand this anymore."

Annie zipped up three of the four open suitcases and began hauling them, one by one, into the walk-in closet in the master bedroom.

"I can do that later," I said. "You don't have to do that."

"Cat, I'm an anal retentive Virgo. Yes, I have to do it."

She stood in front of the last suitcase and I raised my hand to stop her. "Wait a second."

"What?"

"Thank you, Annie, for everything."

"Cat, I'm really sorry you're going through this. I know you're not yourself and you haven't been for a while, even though you're really good at covering up." She paused and continued, "I've never known you to lose your way, to stumble even once or ask anyone for help. You're like…like Wonder Woman. It's nice to see that you're human too. I'm just happy I can do this for you. I'm glad you asked me for help."

My eyes welled up. I could feel a tear sliding down my cheek. Annie bent over and hugged me.

"Annie?" I said, my voice muffled on her shoulder.

"Yeah?"

"Don't tell anyone, okay?"

"Your secret is safe with me." She stood up, threw her head back and laughed, "I'll just go hang up your cape and bodysuit in the closet now."

"Don't forget the bracelets."

Annie smiled and reached for the fourth and final suitcase, my small, well-worn red *valigia*. She bent down to lift it, expecting it to be full, and was surprised when she lost her balance. It was empty.

"What the—? Cat, what do you have in here?"

"Dreams."

CHAPTER 15:

CATCH YOU ON THE REBOUND

I could be your rebound guy. I'm willing to take that chance. —Peter

I fell in love with Peter before I met him. He posted a photo that showed him in profile, leaning against a boulder. Head tilted, brown hair tousled, eyes staring into the distance, he looked rugged and a bit aloof. He'd just competed in an Ironman competition. Please God, I thought, don't let him be the strong, silent type.

God heard me that time. Peter proved to be smart and funny, at least on-line. He also had a lot to say. At last, I thought, a man I can talk to or at least write to. But everyone looks good on paper. In person, it's another story. Editing with a keystroke ensures perfection. The longer my written relationship with Peter wore on, the more he became my idea of perfection, and I his. I guess that's why we avoided the dreaded first phone call for three weeks. We preferred to live with our illusions.

During those three weeks we built up quite a history of shared thoughts, ideas and inside jokes. We also shared greeting cards, tokens of affection and little books we each knew the other would enjoy—all sent by Cupid's stand-in, the Internet. "Cat, when you need a quiet place," read one inscription in a book on daily meditations.

Even though it was digital, there was still something a bit old-fashioned about the way we were going about courting. The buildup to the inevitable first phone call was fraught with delicious tension. The time between the last e-mail and the first date is always a bit scary. What if he sounded like Popeye? What if his eloquence is limited to the page? Would I live up to his expectations? Would he live up to mine?

Peter arrived at the restaurant for our first date carrying white tulips tied with a royal blue satin ribbon, my favorite combination of colors. He had paid attention during our on-line conversations, and now he was being thoughtful.

"Cat, is everything okay?" he asked as he stepped back from our greeting, the standard French two-cheek kiss.

I saw a beautiful life pass before me in those opening seconds. I started to plan our future. Did he just squeeze my hand?

As we waited for our table I took my first really good look at him. Whereas Gabriel was five foot eleven, buff and perfectly proportioned, Peter was tall and lithe. Six feet three inches of lean muscle, he was one tall drink of water.

I felt dizzy looking up into his hazel eyes. Or maybe it was just the pheromones, I wasn't quite sure. He had an open and sincere smile that reached those eyes. Trusting was the word that came to my mind.

If this were a movie instead of a book, I'd insert "cut to" scenes of our first, second and third dates here. What a whirlwind. They all happened in the same first weekend. Cut to: Cat and Peter going for a walk on Mont Royal with its sweeping view of Montreal below. Cut to: Cat and Peter making dinner and dancing to Motown tunes in the kitchen. Cut to: Cat and Peter attending the Holgate exhibit at the Museum of Fine Arts, heads together in quiet conversation.

"So what did you think of the exhibit?" I asked as I peered over the top of my coffee mug in the museum's café.

"I like Holgate's landscapes the best. He really captures the essence of Quebec. There's one that reminds me of my place in the Laurentians. I have a cabin up there. I'd like to show it to you someday."

He was already contemplating a possible weekend getaway. How romantic! A rustic cabin in the woods, a four-poster bed covered in his grandmother's antique quilt and a lazy Sunday spent in bed reading the paper and talking. I could just picture it.

"And you?" he asked, interrupting my fantasy.

"Huh?"

"What did you like best?"

"Oh, right. I liked his nudes. They were real women with real bodies. They reminded me of me," I said coyly.

His eyes gave me the once-over. "Hmmm, I wouldn't know about that. I'm afraid I'm just going to have to reserve comment for another time. But I think Holgate would have been lucky to have you as a model."

I swallowed hard. I still wasn't used to such personal compliments from strangers, but I could tell he meant it.

"Thanks."

Peter was cautious, and who could blame him? I was new at this and he had every reason to be wary. Our physicality thus far was limited. Our first date had ended with a chaste peck on the lips. All of the action of our second date concentrated itself in a prolonged embrace as we danced to Marvin Gaye's "Sexual Healing." Now, on our third date, a very dignified tour of a museum, my nerve endings were vibrating with anticipation. I so wanted to touch and be touched by this man. I didn't realize it at the time, but because it had been years since I felt this kind of desire, it could have been any man.

As we walked down Sherbrooke Avenue he pointed out various buildings, their styles, the dates they were built and the architects who designed them. He had wanted to be an architect, but like many men of our generation he'd ended up marrying his pregnant girlfriend instead and putting his dreams on hold. Now he was settled, with no desire to pursue anything except maybe retirement.

"But if that was your dream, and you now have the time..." I suggested.

"Oh I've thought about it. I even looked into some courses. Maybe someday. Right now there's league hockey in the winter, fishing in the summer and Ironman training. It takes all of my time."

At the time, though I didn't know why, I was slightly disappointed by his lack of ambition. His satisfaction with the status quo reminded me of Gabriel, whom I felt to be rudderless. But maybe he just felt contentment with the way things were. Maybe Gabriel was right, I thought. Maybe I am never happy.

No, I thought. I am happy; it's just that I'm never satisfied. Life is all about learning and growing, not about drifting. Would I end up pushing Peter like I used to push Gabriel to do more and be more?

"And this one," he said, interrupting my thoughts, "is the most beautiful of all."

We stood in front of a Tim Horton's donut shop.

"What? You're joking."

"Yes, I am. But it's still the most beautiful building on the street because of one very unique feature." I glanced at the façade and found nothing remotely interesting in its construction.

"It's because you're in front of it." He gently turned me by my shoulders so I was facing him. And then he kissed me.

I felt my knees go weak for the first time since Dave Cutler had kissed me at the Sigma Nu keg party over 20 years earlier. Gabriel had never kissed me like that. My heart beat against my ribs like a trapped bird trying to flee its cage, and there was a rushing noise in my ears. It was like someone had flipped a switch inside me. I was transported back in time and I was a girl again. Everything in me went molten. If this was just a kiss I couldn't wait for the rest.

That weekend I did most of the talking and he did most of the listening. Twenty years of marriage had me all wound up, and I unwound on the first attentive person to come along. It turns out I experienced a lot of firsts with Peter. Romantically speaking, I cut my teeth on his heart.

"You know," he said cautiously at one point during the weekend. "I could be your rebound guy."

I put up my hand in protest and he grabbed it and placed a kiss in my palm as if giving me a gift. "But I'm willing to take that chance," he continued. "I mean, I would understand if I was. We've all been there."

"What? No way, that's not me," I protested. I had decided early on that I was not going to be just like everyone else. I was going to skip the rebound-guy step.

Divorced for eight years with two grown sons, Peter's last relationship had ended two years earlier. As he explained it, it basically died of "benign neglect." Now he was looking for a serious relationship.

So was I, I reassured him.

"Okay." He looked at me and smiled. Trust. I could see he was going to take me at my word.

Our interlude started a week later on the following Thursday night. It was a long weekend. Two sharp raps of the knocker and I knew it was time to go. I felt like I had just run a marathon. I was out of breath and my pulse raced. Anticipation is a powerful aphrodisiac.

I looked at the little red suitcase in the corner of the closet. "Not this time," I said to it apologetically. "This weekend may be R-rated and I don't think you're quite ready for that."

I looked at my more practical overnight bag that contained clothes that were perfect for a weekend get away at his family cottage up north. I had it all covered from warm fleece jackets to hot lingerie. And an artbook from the Holgate exhibit as a host gift.

I wasn't sure I was quite ready for it either. I was going to sleep with a man who wasn't my husband. Even though I was legally divorced I felt like I was doing something illicit.

Later that night, I rolled over on my side and faced Peter. "It really wasn't a bad marriage. It just wasn't a good one. I wanted more. I know exactly what I want and I'm not going to settle for less. I would prefer to fall truly, madly, deeply in love and have it be extraordinary. I'd rather it last for three days than settle for 20 years of mediocrity. I would be happy with that." (Eish, I cringe sometimes when I remember some of the things that I said.)

"I hope you don't mean that, Cat," he said. "It would be very sad to be satisfied with only three days of love. What you're looking for is more like a shooting star. Wouldn't you rather have the constancy of the sun?"

Constancy? I thought. My entire love life to that point was one long constant drizzle. I had lived in the London of love. Now I wanted heat and sweat and lust. I wanted the fireworks, excitement and passions of Paris.

On the drive back from St. Sauver, he whistled contentedly to himself. I, on the other hand, was feeling a bit restless. It seemed like after a month of getting to know each other, we'd said all we had to say. Or at least I had. To me, he and I had made a journey and arrived at our destination. I was sated, and he wanted more. He mentioned a couple of upcoming barbeques and asked if I would like to go. I said yes, but I knew that meeting his friends would be wrong. Commitments to any further plans would just make it harder for the inevitable. I didn't want a relationship, at least not then, and as great as Peter was I didn't want one with him.

In the days ahead I let our communication taper off before finally meeting him for coffee, where I tearfully explained that he'd been right all along: he was my rebound guy.

He was polite and distant. I couldn't blame him. His lack of recrimination only made me feel worse. As I left the café I wondered about rebound relationships. Did they involve karma? Does what goes around come around? How would the universe extract payment for my selfishness?

It wouldn't be long before I found out.

CHAPTER 16:

THE DEEP END OF THE DATING POOL

What you have is a good case of the guilts. —Annie Lachance

"I have a disease," I practically yelled over the happy hour din. A couple of heads turned in my direction and I flushed red.

Annie took a long drag on her cigarette and exhaled the smoke slowly. "You do not have a disease." She motioned to a waiter to bring her an ashtray.

"I'm sure of it. It feels like a yeast infection but ten times worse."

Annie shook her head and smiled. "Did you use a condom?"

"Yes."

"Then you do not have a disease."

"That's what you think. They're not 100 percent effective, you know. It even says so on the box. I checked, and Web MD says I have the symptoms for at least three STDs."

"What you have," Annie paused and took a sip of her Coke, "is a good case of the guilts. Good girl has sex and must pay."

"It's not that. I have nothing to feel guilty about."

"You know what your problem is?"

"No, but I have a feeling you're going to tell me," I said.

"What you're going through at 45 is what you should have been experiencing in your 20s. All of the exploration, the angst, the anxiety? All that should be behind you, but you're just getting started. You just don't know it."

"How did you get to be so wise?"

"I remember being where you are now. Only you went right from university to marrying the first handsome French Canadian to sweep you off your feet, right?"

Our roles were reversed; who was mentoring who now? "How old were you when…you know." I drew circles in the air with my hands.

"You mean when I first had sex?" Annie mimed the air circles back and laughed. "Eighteen."

"Wow. I was 24 and Gabriel was it. I think I have a lot of catching up to do. Still, I'm sure I have a disease."

"If you're so worried about it, go get tested," she said.

"I did," I offered enthusiastically.

"*And*?"

"Everything came back negative."

Annie threw up her hands. "Waiter!" She stopped the young man passing our table. "Bring me some rum for this Coke, *s'il vous plait*."

It wasn't karma. Turns out I was allergic to the latex.

I learned a lot about myself that first year I spent dating, besides the fact that I was allergic to latex. I subscribed to two Internet dating services, signed up for the friends-and-family plan of fix-me-ups, i.e., blind dates. I also registered for one matchmaking service. Sixty-five first dates later, I had learned two things. First, finding Mr. Right is a numbers game. Second, when you do find Mr. Right and it doesn't work out, don't blame yourself.

My Internet profile listed the theatre as one of my interests, so it was only natural that Richard the Third's (third because he was my third Internet date) introductory e-mail missive opened with a line from Shakespeare's *Love's Labour's Lost.*

Fair Kate/Cat:
From women's eyes this doctrine I derive:
They sparkle still the right Promethean fire;
They are the books, the arts, the academes,
That show, contain, and nourish all the world.

Shakespeare is one of my favorite authors so I was charmed and delighted by Richard's opening lines. We quickly connected by phone and made arrangements for a date at a nearby café, where a short, portly Richard, with facial hair befitting the Bard himself, made his entrance with a flourish. He was wearing a gold-trimmed black cape and a red Kangol golf cap, which he swiped from his head while making a low bow before me. It was an odd combination of Elizabethan pageantry and modern gallantry.

"M'lady," he said.

"Kind sir," I replied.

Wow, this could be fun. But when he insisted on conducting our entire conversation in iambic pentameter, I knew he wasn't the man for me. I should have seen it coming; there is no happy ending to the play either. The princess and her ladies do not end up with their men.

I met man after man who dazzled me with his charms. Could this be him? I wondered. So soon? They were good-looking, wealthy and well educated but they were also cheap and rude to waiters. In the beginning I thought they would improve over time, but that happens only with wine.

Two men flew across the country and two crossed an ocean to spend time with me. In the moment I was flattered. It took all four occasions for me to realize that these were men with more dollars than sense and each one was just looking for a new and unique experience.

Bryan, a media exec, blew in from Los Angeles one fine June weekend. Never married, he was all flash and cash and very full of himself.

"I hope you don't mind, but I'd feel more comfortable if you stayed in a nearby hotel until we got to know each other better," I said. I didn't want to repeat my Peter experience and get too involved too soon.

"Cat, I'm a tall, good-looking man with a lot of money. I don't have to fly 3,000 miles to sleep with a woman. Just find me a nice boutique hotel nearby, preferably a place with high thread-count sheets. I'd like to feel at home."

He didn't want to sleep with me. He wanted to impress me. Coming from Lotus Land, he wanted an audience, an admirer, not a partner. His on-line profile had read, "Wanted: someone to love and adore." He'd left off a very important word at the end of the line: *me.*

Unfortunately, I didn't fare much better with a greasy oilman from Calgary who spent the entire weekend shopping for himself; a wealthy Dutch trader who wanted to go Dutch on everything once he arrived; and a charming Scotsman. I think he was charming but I can't be sure because his Highlander accent was so thick I understood only every fourth word. It was like static on a radio.

Yes, I confess, in the beginning I made allowances for behavior I wouldn't accept in a friend, let alone a stranger. There! I said it. How humiliating. Was I so needy, starved for attention and lonely that I accepted in a stranger behavior I wouldn't tolerate in my marriage? Yes, I guess I was, but that quickly changed the minute I stopped taking things so seriously. I decided to have fun. I didn't approach every date as if it were my last and every man as if he were my only chance for happiness. In my age group—middle-aged baby boomers—there were plenty of available men out there. I just had to meet them. And I did. I also came up with a law.

"Let me get this straight," Annie said as she tucked her long legs under her and settled herself on my cream-colored Natuzzi couch. "You've created a law?"

"Yes. I call it the Law of Thirds."

"You know math was never your strong suit."

"It's simple math, Annie. If you break down 100 percent into equal thirds, you get 33.3, 33.3 and 33.3 percent. In the first 33 percent—"

"Wait a minute!" Annie interrupted. "What happened to the extra 0.3 percent in each third?"

"Let's put that one percent aside for now. I'll come back to that later. The first 33 percent of the time, you meet a man and think he's great, but he doesn't feel the same way."

"Yeah, it sure sucks when he doesn't call for a second date, especially if you think the first went well," Annie said, shaking her head.

"Tell me about it. You know Roberta, right? She and her husband, Sam, fixed me up with one of Sam's colleagues. It was sort of a double date. According to Roberta, 'All I had to do is show up in my bitchin' boots and a skirt, and the rest would take care of itself.' And she was right."

"Kind of like a date with training wheels," Annie said.

"Exactly. But after drinks they left us on our own. It was a wonderful night of good food, good wine and good conversation. We had so much in common I was sure there would be a second date."

"And he never called back?"

"No, and neither Roberta nor I ever found out why."

"All I can say is that if he doesn't know a good thing when he sees one, then he's not the guy for you," Annie said.

"In the second 33 percent of the dating pool," I continued, "he thinks you're the next best thing since golf and a Grey Goose martini, but alas, he doesn't do it for you. So you dance around the idea of a next date and tell him you'll be in touch. Or you let a matchmaking agency take care of it for you."

"And I suppose you tried one of those?" Annie asked.

I told Annie about my experience with Ms. Match. The name should have been my first clue. I put on my best Parisian accent and gave a perfect imitation of Ms. Match herself, a tall, willowy woman with close-cropped white hair who had peered at me over her bright blue Dolce & Gabbana bifocals and said, "You realize, Madame, we're not just any matchmaking service. We are *zee* experts. We guarantee *zee* results. We have *zee* best screening system."

I had squirmed a bit in my chair. I had just completed a battery of compatibility and psychological tests and handed over a hefty check. The song "What I Did for Love" from the musical *A Chorus Line* was running through my head. I hoped she was right.

"It's very simple," she had continued. "You go on *zee date*. And *zhen* you speak to me. *Zere* will be no awkward moments. I take care of *zat*. If it's a match I will let you know. If not, you move on to someone else."

The arrangement had appealed to me: no messy endings for me or the date, and I'd have a definitive answer one way or another regarding a next date. I hated being put on the spot when I didn't feel like meeting the gentleman in question again.

The matchmaker had found Pierre. An actuary, he studied statistics at Concordia University. After all of those compatibility tests I was a bit disappointed that *zee* service matched me up with a numbers guy. Positive thoughts, I had said to myself as I walked into the restaurant. It's important to remain open. He may have an interesting hobby.

Pierre was a bit nondescript, except for his clothes. He wore a navy suit that was slightly rumpled, a white shirt and a red tie. I'm struggling hard as I write this to get an impression of his face, but he left none—at least none that I can remember.

On the bright side, even though he was another French Canadian, I had been led to believe he spoke English. Communicating was hard enough; I wanted someone who was comfortable in English from the get-go. In reality the only English words Pierre knew were numbers. And so we spoke French, which wasn't so bad considering that he was a "*oui/non*" man. No matter how open-ended the question, he answered either yes or no. Luckily I was adept at keeping up both ends of the conversation.

"The agency mentioned you just returned from vacation," I had started.

"Yes." Pierre turned his head slightly to look past my right shoulder.

"Where did you go?" I asked, leaning on my right elbow so I could slide into his field of vision. I hate it when someone doesn't look me in the eye.

"Whistler," he answered, still staring past my shoulder. I turned and looked. There was a wall behind me.

"Really?" I asked. "I'm going to take a flyer here, but since it's February I'm thinking it would be safe to say that you went . . ." In the ensuing pause, I filled in the blank for him while he still stared past my shoulder. "*Ski-ing*?" I drew the word out as my elbow slid farther still and fell right off the table. I jerked myself back in front of him. He didn't seem to notice.

"Yes."

I wanted to cup my hand under his chin and turn his head so we could be face to face, but I resisted the temptation.

"Skiing in BC. That must have been a great experience. I'm not much of a skier. How is it different than skiing here in Eastern Canada?"

"Less icy."

Less icy? All I could think of was that this was the tip of the iceberg of one long, chilly conversation that I feared would never end. But it appeared my probing questions and witty repartee were enough to make Pierre want to prolong the conversation.

"Can I get you another glass of wine?" the waitress asked.

We answered at the same time. Me: "No." Pierre: "*Oui.*"

I had then proceeded to cover a whole host of topics I thought might be of interest to him. I once worked for an insurance company and was able to ask questions about his job. I told stories and poked fun at some of the interesting situations in which I had found myself while traveling. I did my best to make it an entertaining conversation. But by the end I was exhausted; I'd never worked so hard in my life. It was obvious to me that Pierre needed someone a bit less animated and perhaps more reserved. Maybe he was the type who liked to sit in companionable silence?

We had said goodbye in the vestibule of the restaurant. I resolved to call Ms. Dolce & Gabbana in the morning and give her a piece of my mind. There would be no second date. Humph, *zo* much for *zee* screening system. Love, I concluded, could not be calculated by a questionnaire.

"This was fun," Pierre had suddenly said. "I know I'm not supposed to ask but I'd like to do this again. Would you?"

"Wait a minute! He was breaking the rules *and* putting you on the spot," Annie interrupted.

"Tell me about it. He caught me off guard, and I blurted out a vehement 'No.'"

"Well, at least you were honest," Annie said.

"The last 33 percent is the easiest," I concluded. "You both can tell the truth without having to worry about hurt feelings. You can relax and have fun, and you might even end up with a friend."

"So in this last scenario, neither one of you feels there's any potential, so you've got nothing to lose, right?" Annie asked.

"That's it. That's what happened with this guy from Spokane. He looked like a blond Pillsbury Doughboy with sandals. He moved to Montreal along with his electric bike. He was all about peace and love and recycling. 'Cat,' he said halfway through our cappuccinos, 'you're very nice, but I really don't think this will work.' He was right and that was the end of that."

"Yes, but where does all this dating leave you?" Annie asked.

"It leaves you with that elusive one percent where the feelings are mutual."

CHAPTER 17:
THAT ELUSIVE ONE PERCENT

I like it when you talk dirty. —Adrio

Montreal's Crescent Street is not a place I normally frequent. There are too many tourists and stunning 30-somethings, like Annie Lachance, walking around in skinny jeans and camisoles. And I certainly wouldn't go there during Formula One race week with temperatures averaging in the high 90s and thousands of people from everywhere bumping and grinding against each other as they try to get a table on one of the many impromptu sidewalk terraces.

During race week in Montreal, checkered flags are draped across the downtown core like limp laundry on a clothesline. Crowds spill onto the sidewalks and into the streets, where traffic moves at a crawl. The locals cruise down St. Catherine Street and show off their own Ferraris, Lamborghinis, Porches and Maseratis. Busy side streets magically become pedestrian walkways with sound stages from which radio DJs broadcast the action live. Several F1 race cars parked on Crescent Street draw crowds of onlookers. It's the event of the year, an event I'm usually determined to avoid.

"What's with the face?" I asked Annie as she strode into my apartment and flopped into a nearby chair. She extended her long, tanned legs in front of her.

"I've decided not to see Jacques anymore."

Her eyes were red from crying. The elusive Jacques Croquet, ladies' man about town, confirmed bachelor and the one challenge Annie Lachance couldn't master. She'd broken up with Jacques before, but this time there was something different in her demeanor. This time she looked like she meant it. She had given up.

"I can't stay home. Not tonight. Let's go out," she said, her face brightening.

"How about a movie?"

"Cat, I may as well just go home to a cold, dark bedroom."

"Okay, okay, but only till midnight and then I'm calling it quits."

"Done. Cat, if you didn't exist, I'd have to invent you."

"Yeah, right, you're just saying that because it's 100 degrees out there and you know I hate crowds. Where are we going?"

"Newtown," she said.

"Oh God, we'll be right in the thick of it." I glanced down at my attire. Since I wasn't especially interested in making anyone's acquaintance, my look that evening was more casual than Montreal chic. I was wearing a pair of white Capris and a royal blue halter-top. At least I felt cool.

A short while later in the bar at Newtown, I positioned myself on the terrace near an open door but within the orbit of the wait staff. Fresh air and cold drinks: what more could a girl ask for? As someone who travels frequently for business and often dines alone, I'm comfortable in the role of detached observer. The self-consciousness I might have felt in such a situation had disappeared many years ago.

A few feet away I could see that the lovely Annie had struck up an animated conversation with a stylish young man. I glanced at my watch; it was 11:45 p.m. I sighed contentedly. My work here was done. I was free to go with 15 minutes to spare, time off for good behavior. Or so I thought.

It was one of those classic cinematic moments when the leading lady glances across the room and her eyes meet those of the handsome leading man.

He smiled at me and my heart skipped a beat. He was chatting with a friend but he spent the next ten minutes making eye contact and smiling at me. I made sure to reciprocate. I was getting impatient when suddenly he started to walk right toward me. At last.

Crisp white linen shirt, dress pants: he was so cool and fresh-looking. Tall, dark hair and eyes, swarthy skin: he was exotic and just my type. I watched him approach and then surprisingly pass me by on the way to the gents.

What?!

Nonplussed, I thought he'd catch me on the return, but he didn't. He went straight back to his table. What was he up to? Did I misread the signals?

Suddenly, from out of nowhere, two tall blonds in their 30s walked over to his table and struck up a conversation. It was that easy, but as a 40-something, let-the-guy-make-the-first-move kind of gal, I hadn't even considered it. But now I reconsidered.

I made a quick calculation. I wasn't there trolling for a man. I didn't know anyone in the bar besides Annie. I had nothing to lose. Why not go for the bold gesture? When he glanced my way again while the others at his table were engaged in animated conversation, I crooked my index finger in a "come hither" movement, lowered my chin and smiled mischievously. It was a calculated risk. He could accept the invitation or he could choose to ignore it. If he accepted, it would be an interesting night. If he rejected it, no one would be the wiser but me.

He accepted. He picked up his drink, excused himself and walked over to my table. "You beckoned?" he asked.

"I had no choice. You were making eye contact with me all night and then you totally ignored me. And what's with the fly-by?" I nodded in the direction of the toilet.

He laughed. "I guess I lost my nerve. I really didn't think you'd be interested in me."

Was he kidding? I extended my hand. "Cat."

"Adrio."

"I can't quite place the accent."

"Brazil."

"What do you do?"

"I'm a pilot."

"Oh God, that remark about the fly-by." I leaned my head against the wall.

"It was perfect."

"I can't believe I said that."

"Neither can I. You're very good."

"Total coincidence."

"I don't think so."

"What airline?"

"Private pilot. Corporate jets." He paused to let me take in that bit of impressive information.

"Hmmm, heavy iron. Fokker?" Now it was his turn to be surprised.

"I like it when you talk dirty." There was that smile again.

"No, I bet it's a Falcon? Maybe a Piaggio? Or a Gulfstream?"

A confused look crossed his face. "Falcon. How did you know? Are you in the aviation business?"

He was intrigued. After all, it isn't every day you stumble across a woman who can name the world's four or five best-selling private aircraft.

"I used to be. A long time ago."

I toyed with him a while before I let him in on my ad agency background. I explained that my main account had been a corporate aircraft manufacturer. I remembered enough aviation-speak to impress him and myself. We made a date to meet the next day for lunch to continue the conversation.

The next day we met in the charming Pointe Claire Village on the edge of Lac St-Louis. It was the perfect counterbalance to the heat and crowds of St. Catherine Street the previous night. Blue skies, billowy clouds and a spectacular view of the lake. We watched as an exuberant wedding party burst through the doors of St-Joachim de Pointe Claire Church into the dazzling sunshine.

There are so many things I remember about that first weekend together. Adrio's discrete and dignified donation to a homeless man and the observation that it's not just the lack of money that keeps us one step away from the street. At first I thought he was trying to impress me, except he actually talked to the man like a human being rather than just paying him to go away.

Unlike Gabriel, he exuded patience and good humor when confronted with an impromptu shopping scenario. He chatted up the store owners while I made a quick change from the chic black outfit I wore (much too hot for that day) to a more suitable, barely there summer dress made in Brazil, of all places. I still have that dress, and every time I wear it I'm reminded of that weekend.

"Look," he said as he dropped me off at my apartment. "I know we just met and God knows where this will go, and I'm totally unreliable when it comes to relationships, but I had such a good time, I hate for it to end. I don't want to presume, but I'd like it if you could stay with me tonight. I'm at the Hilton. Just call and I'll pick you up."

It was sudden and, with Detroit as his home base, the odds of our seeing each other on a regular basis weren't great. But I wanted to live this experience—all of it. Maybe we could beat the odds. But then I thought better of it. My last distance relationship hadn't turned out all that well.

I did my best to keep busy around the apartment, but no matter how hard I tried, my eyes kept straying to my cell phone on the kitchen counter. I was about to dial his number when it rang. There was no greeting, just a question.

"Do you have candles?"

"What? Yes."

"And bubble bath?"

I could see where this was heading. It was shaping up to be a Calgon moment. Take me away, Adrio, I thought.

"I did some shopping after I left you. I picked up some champagne and strawberries. Too many for me to eat by myself. Do you care to join me?"

I will always have a soft spot in my heart for the Hilton. Every time I drive past it I recall that intensely sunny Sunday morning in vivid detail. I awoke in a tangle of rumpled sheets feeling very happy, a darkly handsome man in a captain's uniform standing over me, smiling.

Adrio had to fly some tycoon to his home in White Plains, New York, but he would be back in time for dinner. He kissed me on the top of my head and handed me his pass to the executive lounge. "Breakfast," he said in a commanding voice, "is the most important meal of the day." And then he pulled a dark chocolate bar from his pocket and handed it to me for later in case I missed him.

And so it went for most of the summer. In actual fact there were only a handful of weekends that we spent together because Adrio was always on call. I lived for those hourly, daily and ultimately weekly text messages, e-mails and Skype calls that linked us in Montreal and Cannes, Montreal and Sardinia, Montreal and Prague. When Adrio came to Montreal we made the most of those weekends. I became a tourist in my own city.

We played house, but a house is not a home. I could understand Adrio's paradoxical nature as well as my own. He wanted to be at home when he was traveling, and he longed for the open skies when he was home for too long. That broke up his first marriage and prevented him from contemplating another. The stay/go paradox, it was one of the few things we shared. Rather than drive us apart, that same paradox had kept Gabriel and me married for so long. And so, in a way, Adrio was perfect for me. The intensity of those meetings and leave takings was like a drug, and I was always waiting for my next fix.

Some of my more cynical girlfriends thought perhaps Adrio was married. I knew he was married to his job. I was his mistress, what Julia Roberts' character in *Pretty Woman* once referred to as a "beck-and-call girl." In the end, it wasn't the infrequency of meeting that proved our undoing. I could have continued until one or the other of us changed our mind and/or our situation. No. In the end, it was the planning and miscommunication that was the problem.

It sounds like a cliché given his choice of profession, but Adrio is flighty, and he would be the first to admit it. He told me it's a common trait among pilots. His checklist before he walks out the door is: Spectacles. Testicles. Wallet. Watch. He had more flexibility with his time and his money than I did, and I began to resent his inconsistency. Because he worked for a major corporation and his schedule was unpredictable, I made accommodations to a point. But I had a job and a life too.

Last-minute changes after reservations were made and tickets were bought were a common occurrence. The first time it happened was due to a technical difficulty and a miscommunication because his BlackBerry died. The second time he had to hook up with another pilot, a buddy he saw often but whom he wanted to get together with anyway because he happened to be in Montreal the same weekend. (I wasn't invited.) The third time he picked up an extra flight and ducked out early on a weekend to fly an R&B legend back to Motown, then stayed there because it's his home base.

In the end I realized I wasn't a priority. I was a fly-by. I wanted more.

"Hi sweetie," I yelled over a bad connection. And no wonder. He was calling from a pool bar somewhere in Barbados. "I've made the reservations. I'll see you in Barcelona on the fourth."

"That's what I wanted to talk to you about," he yelled back. "I won't be able to get there until the 11th. I have a meeting with my real estate agent in Cyprus. I have to look at some property."

"That's going to be a problem. I can't change the ticket. It's high season and I had a hard time getting this flight in the first place."

"Well, why don't you go early and stay at the hotel? Use my points and it won't cost you a thing."

"By myself? Why bother?"

"Think of it as a vacation. I'll join you as soon as I can. Maybe I can make it before the 11th."

"Adrio, if I wanted to take a vacation by myself, I'd go to Paris. You can't keep doing this. I have a job and a life. I moved things around to accommodate the dates you gave me last week."

Except for the pool noise in the background, there was silence on his end.

"I can't do this anymore," I said.

"Wait, does this mean you're not going then?"

"Goodbye, Adrio."

In the end, that one percent proved to be very elusive indeed.

CHAPTER 18:
A CASE OF PREMATURE INFATUATION

You're not born into class. You either have it or you don't. —Grandma Vi

Howard and I met on a local Internet dating site and exchanged a week's worth of e-mails before meeting. It was early on a Saturday evening when I called him to organize coffee for the following week.

"Next week?" he said, clearly disappointed. "If neither one of us has plans, why can't it be tonight?"

I thought about it, then said, "Why not? Okay, you're on."

We agreed to meet for a drink in the garden courtyard of the über-hip Bice. He was everything I was looking for: local, a business owner and hot. His wavy brown hair had a hint of grey at the temples. His broad chest and flat belly clearly indicated that he worked out regularly. He was also incredibly gracious to everyone, from the restaurant owner to the teenage busboy who cleared the table. Drinks turned into dinner, which turned into a late-night conversation that closed the place and finished up on Mont Royal where we watched the sunrise.

We were raised with similar family backgrounds and basic values. He was one of four brothers. Our fathers had each played a significant role in our respective lives. Howard and his dad were business partners, and my dad would usually mind his own business unless you asked him not to.

"What do you think about a nice Jewish boy like me and a good Catholic girl like you getting together?" he asked.

"I think the collective guilt might kill us," I responded.

We both laughed at a stereotype we knew to be true, at least for us. We made out like teenagers in the back seat of his car while listening to Eddie Money on the stereo. "Baby Hold On." It was 1978 all over again—the last year of high school with nothing but the future ahead of us.

By morning we'd built up quite an appetite, so we decided to continue our conversation over breakfast.

"So do you think I could be boyfriend material?"

I hesitated before answering. "Well, I'd certainly like to find out."

A few days later we met for dinner at a café in my neighborhood.

"I had dinner with the guys last night and I told them all about you."

"Really? What did you say?"

"Only how great you are. A little bit about what you do. Your travels. They were impressed and so am I. Maybe even a bit intimidated."

"Oh please, if I were intimidating we wouldn't be having this conversation, now would we?"

Howard confessed that he had hesitated asking me out for our fourth date. He was a man obsessed with his lawn, his new driveway, his rims, building a new deck, and finding the right summer camp for his kids. He was worried I would be bored with his lifestyle. Because my job in international sales took me on the road a good bit of the time, I was used to living the high life, as he pointed out to me.

"Hmmm." I said. "Anyone who travels for a living and spends half of his or her life waiting in long lines at airport security knows just how glamorous life on the road can be. Please."

He also felt that because I didn't have the responsibilities of children and a house, I wouldn't be able to relate to him.

"I don't think you necessarily have to have your own children to be able to relate to them, but what do I know?" I said. And, I thought, I wasn't about to try and convince a man who has already made up his mind.

It was early days, and we weren't all that invested in each other; I told him I'd understand if he wanted to bow out. I appreciated his honesty, and while it would be disappointing, it was okay. It was for the best, really, because I was busy preparing for an upcoming sales trip that would take me to Johannesburg, Nice, Frankfurt, London and, finally, Dublin, where I planned to spend time with family.

The minute I said all this, Howard did an about-face and made a counter-argument. He felt that our different interests could coexist nicely. "You know," he said, "you could read while I puttered around the garden. You could tell me about the books you're reading. I do read the financial papers; I could help you with your investments. Maybe someday I could travel with you. I went to Cancun once. Maybe we could go together? And I think the fact you don't have kids means we don't have to worry about blending families. You know how competitive kids can be."

I wasn't convinced; I thought perhaps he'd been right to begin with. We were so different. My experience with Adrio also made me hesitate.

Howard spent the next few weeks proving that he wanted to be boyfriend material. He called on a daily basis to and from his commute to work. He called from the elliptical machine at the gym. When I was on the road we talked daily via Skype. He even phoned my cousin's house in Dublin one afternoon to chat. They were suitably impressed with my "Jewish fella." I couldn't wait to get home to see him. We had a spectacular reunion in the foyer of his house; thankfully the kids were with his ex.

We dined al fresco several times a week at quaint cafés on Prince Arthur, attended performances at the Just for Laughs Comedy Festival and spent weekends just hanging out at my pool. Our conversations ranged from child-rearing challenges (his) to vacation-planning challenges (mine) as I tried to coordinate our hectic schedules for a September getaway.

I was overwhelmed by his attentiveness, but in a good way. Sometimes when I wanted to put on the brakes, he would turn on the charm. He was, after all, a good salesman.

About two months into our relationship, Howard thought it was time I met his kids. Could I come for supper in two hours?

"Two hours? Don't you think it would be better to plan something? You know, give them, and me, a little notice?"

"It's not like they don't know about you."

"It's only been a couple of months. It might be a bit premature."

"Okay. Up to you. But if you want to come over tonight, it's pizza and a movie."

"How about next time you have them? In two weeks?"

"They're off to camp in two weeks. Cat, you're going to have to meet them someday."

When is a good time to meet someone's children? After three months? Six months? Never? If there was a rule of thumb I couldn't find it. I decided to go.

Howard had three great kids: Melanie, 14; Michael, 11; and David, 9. Rounding out our party that evening was Melanie's friend Hillary, who was a bit shy around adults. His kids were fun and funny as they teased their father over dinner. Howard made sure to include Hillary in the conversation as often as possible without making her feel uncomfortable.

As I watched our little group around the table, I could feel what it must be like to have your own family. Imaginary pictures of my own children came to mind, and while I'm not in the habit of second-guessing myself or my choices, I did wonder, if only for a second, how my life would have been different if I'd had children. Not necessarily better, I thought. Just different.

After a cooperative clean-up effort in the kitchen, the kids excused themselves. The girls went upstairs to watch TV while Michael and David went into the den to play on the computer. I decided to join the girls, but not wanting to interrupt them, I paused on the landing to give them a chance to finish a conversation they were having.

"I like your father's new friend. She's nice," Hillary said.

"So do I. But you know my father. He changes girlfriends like he changes his underwear."

They both let out a knowing sigh.

Out of the mouths of babes, I thought. I hoped I'd misheard but the looks on their faces when I walked in the room told me otherwise. Later, when I asked Howard about it, he made a joke. "It's utterly false. You know I don't wear any underwear."

As we drove Hillary home, we took a detour through the neighboring development to look at some of the newly constructed houses.

"What do you think?" he asked.

"They're big."

"I could see you in one of those houses."

"You could?"

He leaned over and whispered in my ear, "You should see the master bedrooms."

"Howard, shush, the kids will hear you."

Looking back on the relationship I would have to say that a lot of what drove it was the physical aspect. More often than not our intimacy was tinged with guilty pleasure because many of our liaisons bordered on the unpredictable. Howard was one of those rare men who took pleasure in giving pleasure. He was an observer and a participant at the same time.

As a male friend of mine once put it, "Exciting a man is like turning on a light switch. For a woman, it's like lighting 100 candles. It takes time but the glow is worth it." When it came to generating heat and light, Howard approached each encounter with a full box of matches.

That summer went by in a blur. I could classify the whole relationship in three phases: a quick start, an impulsive middle and an abrupt end. We were two people in a hurry to get to…where? Our journey was filled with lots of happy pit stops, but in the end we ran out of gas before we could ever agree on a vacation spot, let alone a final destination.

The end of our relationship completely caught me off guard. When I look back on the time we spent together, I either missed whatever signs there were or ignored them because I was enjoying myself so much. This would be especially and ironically true for our last weekend.

We spent a relaxing afternoon by the pool, had a nice lunch and then took a long walk. We were contemplating what to do about dinner—he wasn't due to pick up the kids until nine in the evening—when he suddenly got off the couch and said he had to leave. It was five o'clock. He picked up his bag and headed to the door just like that.

"Is everything all right?" I asked. "Do you feel okay?"

"I've just got to go."

"What about dinner?"

"Can you manage without me?"

"Sure."

"Great, thanks. I'll call you later."

Although his behavior was sudden, I didn't think it all that strange because so much of what we did was spur of the moment. Perhaps he needed some space. I could understand that, and I was prepared to give it to him. But what I couldn't understand was the silence that followed.

The drastic reduction from several phone calls a day to none made me wonder if his behavior was driven by more than the need for space. The perfunctory "Hi, how are you?" phone call came three days later. It was my first glimpse of the gradually disappearing man. I just didn't know it at the time.

He wanted to come over to my place for dinner because the kids were going to be with their mom. I exhaled for the first time in days. I'd grown attached to this man and I believed we would realize all of our plans someday. The problem was that someday had become a moving target. We were impulsive rather than deliberate. Each time we advanced, the plan retreated.

Our dinner together was the beginning of our end. After our usual discussion about the kids and his business, he ran out of things to say. There was tension in the room and no way to release it, and I had a good idea why. I could give him an opening and see where things go, I thought, or I could make him work for it.

Silence is the first sign of rejection. I don't want to talk to you; therefore, I have nothing to say. I'm not talking about companionable silence that is as mutual as it is comfortable, nor am I talking about those quiet moments of reflection when one person has something on his mind. No, the silence of rejection has more to do with weariness and boredom than the silence of just being.

Most of my girlfriends would come down on the side of making a man work to get out of a relationship. I, despite great personal cost, always take the high road. Once, just once, I would love to hurl a dish across the room, throw a drink in a man's face or set fire to his golf clubs in the driveway. But that's not me. Not even close. I just don't have that type of wrath in me. My Grandma Vi once said, "You're not born into class. You either have it or you don't. And you have class." She conducted herself with dignity at all times, and she expected me to do the same.

"Right, what we have here is a failure to communicate," I said. This is a well-known line from the classic movie *Cool Hand Luke*, starring Paul Newman. It's an opening that is meant to keep things light, and is a much better alternative than, "We have to talk."

It made Howard laugh.

"Look, Howard. You bolted out of here on Sunday as if you were being chased. What's going on?" I was hoping for a plausible explanation to his behavior so we could move on, or at least work through it.

"I don't know. I just had to go."

"And now you've barely said ten sentences all night. Talk to me."

"I'm sorry, Cat. I don't know what to say."

I can keep up a good front for only so long. All at once it was clear; he was not going to assuage any of my fears and tell me that everything was fine. It was right about then that my eyes got a bit watery.

"Let me see if I can break it down for you. I figure it's got to be one of three things. One, either I said or did something to upset you." If it was a mere misunderstanding, I could fix that.

"No, it's not that."

I was afraid to put forth my other two conclusions because, deep down, I felt they were closer to the mark. But I went ahead anyway. My eyes may have been watery but at least my voice was steady. I took a deep breath and continued.

"So maybe we were nothing but a house on fire, spontaneous combustion, and now that we've burned ourselves out all that's left are the ashes. Or you've changed your mind about us and you don't know how to tell me."

"I really don't know what it is."

I'm sure he did know but he just wasn't ready to admit it to himself, much less to me. "You're upset; maybe we should talk about it another time," he said.

"It's just that this sudden change has caught me by surprise."

"I better go. I'll call you."

The following week Howard did call me every day but not as often as before. I could tell he was trying to figure out how to make a graceful exit. He didn't have it in him to be a jerk. But neither one of us wanted things to continue in this way; it was too hard, and we both knew we had to wrap things up.

Finally, we agreed to meet at Presse Café. There would be no stray emotions, I assured him. He arrived late. That's how I knew he'd already disengaged from us as a couple. He no longer cared enough about me to be on time.

"Hey," he offered by way of an excuse, "most guys wouldn't even have done this much. They would have just walked away without a word. I'm sorry, Cat. It has nothing to do with you. I guess I just changed my mind."

"Just like that."

Howard looked past me. I was disappointed, bewildered and hurt. I wanted to cry foul. I ran the instant replay in my head, certain that the referee had made a bad call. I'd met his kids. We were planning a holiday.

We enjoyed each other's company. I'd caught a glimpse of the life I'd missed out on with Gabriel. It was right there within reach, and now it had disappeared just like that.

I was also angry, but I wasn't sure why or at whom: him or me? He hadn't really done anything wrong, but I felt like he'd treated me like some trial offer that he was returning after three months for a full refund. No risk and no loss. I sat staring at my full coffee cup. Suddenly it occurred to me that he'd already moved on; perhaps his daughter had been right after all.

I recovered my dignity and a bit of backbone on my way out to the parking lot. He walked me to my car and embraced me. I couldn't return it; what was the point?

I watched his Audi pull out of the parking lot into traffic. That night he would drive his expensive imported car and park it in his driveway in a Montreal suburb. Then he would water his lawn. I would return home and pack for my next trip to South Africa. That's when it hit me. Howard was a regular guy, and regular guys like regular girls. And the last thing I am is a regular girl.

CHAPTER 19:
TWO CAN PLAY AT THAT GAME

What do you expect? We do something nice and you call us chauvinists. We don't do it and you call us rude. What is it with you women? We can't win.—Father Goose

Howard's abrupt departure smarted for a while, but on a gradually diminishing basis. I didn't know it then, but he had done us both a favor. Not getting what I thought I wanted was a good thing. Getting what I needed—a physical connection that not only made me feel good in the moment but left me with a residual sense of well being—was also a good thing. The question was, could I replace just that one aspect of the relationship, the connection, without the emotional complication? There was only one way to find out.

In an effort to work off some of that excess sexual energy that had built up since Howard's hasty departure, I decided to take my sorry self to the gym. I don't dress for the gym; no color-coordinated outfits and no make-up. I usually do my best to blend in with the equipment. My goal is to push myself to exhaustion so when I go home I can fall into bed and a dreamless sleep.

I love this particular gym because the Stairmaster machines are right next to the room with the free weights. And while I like to read on the Stairmaster to pass the time, I'm not above watching the guys pump a little iron. It's a very efficient way to work out my body and my imagination. There's nothing like slick, sweaty men to get my heart going, although I doubt it counts toward my aerobic workout.

It's very difficult to meet men in the gym, despite the fact that they're everywhere. That's because everyone is there for a purpose—to work out—and men and women usually work out in separate areas of the gym. The opportunities to start a conversation are few and far between.

However, I have found quite by accident that certain articles of clothing are interesting yet neutral enough to give a guy the opening he needs to strike up a conversation. I once wore a golf cap with the Masters Golf Tournament logo embroidered on it.

"Nice hat. Did you attend the Masters?" a nice-looking guy asked.

"No, unfortunately I didn't. But I did catch a few rounds on TV." (Yeah right, while I was flicking between the Lifetime and Oxygen channels.)

"Do you golf?"

"Umm, no." (I hate golf.) "But I've always wanted to learn." (He was cute.) "I plan to sign up for lessons." (And I was immediately on the down escalator to hell.)

I live in Montreal, so the most noticeable article of clothing to elicit a comment is something that identifies me as American. In a room filled with locals sporting sweats from McGill, Concordia or the University of Quebec at Montreal, a sweatshirt that says "US NAVY Barber's Point"—a gift from my brother Danny— always gets noticed. It makes it easy for someone to strike up a conversation. It usually begins with the obvious: "Are you American?"

An affirmative answer leads to second, third and fourth questions about where I'm from and what I'm doing in Montreal. And before you know it, I'm having a coffee at the Second Cup next door—although sometimes it's not that easy. Sometimes getting off on the wrong foot can also lead to all sorts of unexpected surprises.

That's how I met Father Goose, a recently divorced father of two teenagers. He and I had a prickly sort of chemistry that told me he would be just the type of guy to drive me crazy both in and out of bed. He was that ubiquitous breed of entitled Italian-Canadian male: doted on by his mother, waited on by his sisters and ignored by his wife. He was too busy taking care of his landscaping business to notice that the last time he and his wife had had a conversation was at his Uncle Guido's funeral six months earlier. He was stunned when she announced she was leaving. What made it worse, he was the last to know.

So it was no wonder he was a little less than chivalrous when we first met. He cut in front of me at the gym's water cooler, then emptied the last of the jug into his bottle and didn't bother to replace it with the full container sitting on the floor. Medium height and powerfully built, he had not an ounce of fat on him. His thick black hair curled at the base of his neck. I resisted the temptation to run my fingers through it.

"Are you always this charming? Or are you making a special effort on my behalf?" I asked.

"What do you expect? We do something nice and you call us chauvinists. We don't do it and you call us rude. What is it with you women? We can't win."

"Ouch, having a bad day are we?"

"It didn't start out that way." He gave me an accusatory look.

"Well, allow me then." I swept my arm out to the side to let him pass. "Don't trip," I said as he walked past me.

You have to love karma. That's exactly what he did. I burst out laughing, and so did he.

"How did you do that?"

"I didn't do a thing, my friend. You did it to yourself."

He paused for a second and looked at me. "You're more right than you know." He returned to the water cooler and put the full jug of water in place.

"Even?"

"Even," I said as we shook hands.

His generalizations about women ticked me off as I'm sure my generalizations about men did him. I was attracted to him, yet at the same time I was put off by his insular and defensive attitude. This combination essentially made him perfect. The heat of the debate continued all the way back to my apartment and ended by our declaring a truce in bed.

I'd found a part-time lover capable of giving me what I needed with no strings attached, a handy guy to have around when I found myself between men. Likewise, since he "couldn't find" the right woman for a steady relationship, I was just right for him.

I'm sure it sounds like a cold and calculated arrangement, but it wasn't. It was a clearly defined deal with no expectations other than a good time a couple of hours a week when the timing was right. It was a very French arrangement. The question was, could I sustain it?

As with most activities—golf, tennis and, yes, sex—there's theory, and there's practice. When it comes to the theory you can operate from an outdated and naive paradigm: sex equals "love," or at the very least, "like." There are new rules to this game and if you don't know them you can get hurt. The number one rule is "don't read into the relationship more than is actually there."

I have bruised my heart on more than one occasion when I chose to ignore that rule, but like a good student, I eventually caught on and learned to appreciate sex in all of its wondrous facets, the way a man does: sex for the sake of sex (hot sex), sex as a release, sex with yourself, synchronistic sex and, finally, sex that is so transcendent that it borders on the spiritual. I did feel like I was walking a fine line because it's not always easy to balance thinking like a man against feeling like a woman. No matter how well I think I can uncouple one from the other, let me say this: there's only one Samantha Jones, and she exists on TV.

As for the practice part, it was both liberating and exhilarating. Suddenly I was glad I wasn't 20 years old. I was 47 and experienced. None of this fumbling about or pretending we knew what we were doing. We did. But I think men at this stage of their lives have to try harder. Physically, their potency is waning while we women are reaching our sexual peak.

I remember one particular lazy Sunday morning while still in bed, a lover asked me if I felt vulnerable when I was naked. On the contrary, I told him. It's when I'm naked in bed with a man that I feel my most powerful. It's outside of the bedroom, when we're both dressed, that I feel the most exposed and most at risk to the vagaries of a man's feelings.

I think men are prone to the same doubts and worries as women, but in a different way. So much of who a man is is tied to what he does. And part of what he does is give and receive pleasure. I once told a married Swedish architect exactly what I wanted and in minute detail. I was being naughty and I knew it. I knew it was going to be a one-off, so I thought, why not? He was so relieved that he didn't have to guess at what would please me that the ease and enjoyment that followed took us both by surprise—so much so that the relationship continued for another five months. In one e-mail he wrote, "I must admit that I felt a little out of practice…I hope, however, that you felt my 'enthusiasm.'" Did I ever.

Physically, sex is a pleasurable experience and it sure beats working out at the gym, but that residual high or afterglow of lovemaking isn't there. I've come to the conclusion that sex for the sake of sex is a lot like "lite" anything. Something is missing. I can't understand how so many men live on a steady diet of it, but then again they drink an awful lot of lite beer. I know now that I need something more filling and fulfilling.

In the meantime, Father Goose would drop by between hockey games, parent–teacher meetings and trips to the gym. We would see each other three or four times a week. He was everything I thought I wanted in a relationship but couldn't have. He was the boy next door, the one I'd avoided my entire life. Sometimes he would stay and we'd talk about his family, his divorce, the wine he was making or the new recipe he'd got from his mother for spaghetti with clam sauce. But I was a spectator in his life; his conversations and his activities never included even a hint of me. He would talk about his dream lover: a petite, dark-haired, dark-skinned woman with doe eyes. She always wore a sexy red dress. He could see them dancing together on a beach on a Caribbean island, just the two of them. I found myself sighing at his descriptions. I envied that woman. Why couldn't I be her?

I dialed back my encounters with Father Goose to once a week, then once every two weeks, then monthly, which was about as long as I could go before I called him. It was far from ideal, but it was better than nothing.

Or at least I thought at the time.

CHAPTER 20:
I TEACH, THEREFORE I AM

Cat, I think you have a brilliant career ahead of you as a teacher. —Sister Mary Grace

So it's not *just* sex, at least not for me. The physical gratification is intense at first, but without feelings to sustain it, it falls flat. I wasn't giving up on Father Goose and our arrangement, but suddenly it didn't seem as essential as I once thought. It became a matter of convenience for us both.

I thought I'd had it all figured out. I'm a smart girl; I know all the answers, right? Then why was I restless? It still felt like something was missing.

I did a quick mental review of all the things I was grateful for:

CAT'S CHECKLIST

- Good health (check)
- Self-esteem/I like who I am (check)
- Great family (check)
- Gratitude (check)
- Spirituality (check)
- Loyal friends (check)
- Rewarding career (check)
- Life in Montreal (check)
- Interests too numerous to mention (check, check, check)

Nothing was jumping out at me. All this fruitless searching was making me a little crazy, so I did what I usually do whenever I am faced with a question or a difficulty I can't solve: I ride my bike.

It was a crisp spring day. The sun was shining and the wind was cold, but it felt good to be out in the fresh air. I soon forgot about Father Goose and all of the worry wasps buzzing around in my brain. I hit a rhythm where bike, rider and nature are one.

Wind is my element. I love the way it touches my body, sometimes soft and gentle, at other times vigorous and strong. It speaks to me when it rustles through the dry autumn leaves, howls during a storm or makes a willow dance. We're friends.

As I rode along the Lachine Canal I found myself transported to a tranquil place. And in the quiet of the moment, I thought I heard it speak to me. It spoke so softly, I nearly missed it. God sends messages and messengers in many different ways. When God sent a message to St. Paul he used a lightning bolt. God found me to be a more attentive listener because the messenger was a bit subtler. It was more like a whisper than a shout and much less dramatic than lightning.

I wasn't sure what I heard. But with each passing mile it became clearer. It started out like the tinkling of a bell and soon became more insistent. And then I saw that I was cycling past a school and the bell was actually a school bell. Class was ending and students were spilling out of the building. For years now, I thought, the universe has given me so many good things. It's also seen me through some tough times, and although I always recognized that fact and was appreciative every single day for every single thing, I was always on the receiving end of things. It was time to give back. That was my Aha! moment that Oprah talks about.

But what was I going to give back? I could write someone a check. That's easy, but you do it at arm's length with a pen stroke. When I was called to make an accounting of myself at the end of my life, what if all I could say was "I donated X to charity"? Would that be good enough?

I had time and talent, but what was I doing with them?

I have always been a teacher, albeit a somewhat reluctant one. Growing up as the oldest of so many siblings, I became a natural teacher, both out of necessity and expediency. The last thing I wanted to do was keep my friends waiting, so it was in my best interest to help create little independent people as quickly as possible. What I didn't realize was how much fun I was having in the process.

Even so, I never wanted to be a teacher when I grew up. As a kid I wanted to be a spy. Why was there no female version of James Bond? Why did James get to have all the fun while poor old Miss Moneypenny stayed behind and answered the phones? The closest I ever got to a role model was in the Queen song "Killer Queen." That was the life I wanted: Moët & Chandon. I wanted to chat up Khrushchev and Kennedy. I wanted perfume from Paris. I wanted to be dynamite with a laser beam.

The high school I attended didn't have any laser beams, so I stuck to languages and basic science. Once in an earth science class I gave a demonstration on soil erosion that was simple and effective. I didn't tell them; I *showed* them how tap water washing away the soil I held in my hands was different from it sprinkling a potted plant. Show, not tell—that was my method. Everyone got it.

"Cat, I think you have a brilliant career ahead of you as a teacher," Sister Mary Grace said in front of the whole class.

"No way!" I spit out the words in the don't-tell-me-what-to-do attitude of every 14-year-old. I was offended, but only publicly. Secretly I was pleased. I was good at teaching and I enjoyed it, but I would never admit it to anyone. Over the years in a professional capacity, I'd trained or lectured on various topics and enjoyed every minute of it. There's no greater satisfaction for me than to see the moment when my students or audience grasp the concept, when a flicker of recognition crosses their faces, and they get it. It's not a lightbulb that goes on over their heads that does it for me; it's the light in their eyes. It's the idea that in some small way I was responsible for that. It's more than a sense of accomplishment; it's a sense of fulfillment.

Now I knew what I had to do. I had to stop fighting myself and start working with my gifts. It was the moment I decided to stop swimming upstream, let go and see where life's current would take me. It wasn't a moment of surrender; it was a moment of acceptance.

I made an appointment to meet with a counselor at the local volunteer bureau to see if I could be matched with an organization that could use my skills as a teacher or as a museum docent. Ironically, of all the matchmaking services I tried over the years, this one yielded the best results. They matched me up with the Chinese Community Cultural Center as an ESL (English as a Second Language) teacher on Saturday mornings. It was the perfect match on several levels. I'd grown up in a working-class Italian immigrant neighborhood and I'd seen how my friends' parents often struggled with their adopted language. It made me realize how hard it is to be a stranger in a strange land.

The fear of being laughed at usually keeps people silent. As someone who has made more than her fair share of linguistic blunders in several languages, I should know. That doesn't stop me, because experience has taught me that most people appreciate my expressive attempts at speaking their language, and they are smart enough to realize that I'd really meant to say "car" and not "chariot" when I'd asked them where they were parked.

In the interest of fair play, I asked my students to teach me a few words or phrases in their language. This immediately put us on a level playing field. It broke down the walls and showed them that if I was willing to put myself out there in a public way, so should they. More often than not we usually shared a good laugh during our classes, mostly at my expense. But I didn't mind. My having a thick skin showed them that it's not all that embarrassing to make a mistake.

Despite all our hard work, I could see that many of my students were still struggling. When I asked if they practiced speaking English on their own, they reluctantly but honestly confessed that they hardly spoke English at all outside the classroom. The diversity of a city like Montreal, just like Canada itself, makes it very easy for immigrants to retain their native languages, customs, cuisine and culture. Most of my students lived in Chinese neighborhoods, shopped at Chinese merchants in Chinatown and socialized with their family and close friends. Very few socialized outside their own community, so there really was no need to go beyond their comfort zone unless they were forced to. So I decided to force them.

I'd accumulated all of this dating knowledge for a reason. It occurred to me that I could apply the concept of speed dating to learning English. After all, what is speed dating but a series of conversations with strangers? This was precisely what my students were missing, so I recruited several of my friends and friends of friends to come to class one morning. We set up the classroom with pairs of chairs. Every eight minutes the guests rotated while the students stayed in place. Every eight minutes each student had the opportunity to speak to a complete stranger and put all of his or her learning into practice. At the end we enjoyed a buffet lunch of some of the best Chinese food I had ever eaten, from handmade noodles with fiddleheads and a spicy shrimp dish as a main course to sesame balls and almond cookies for dessert. The conversations continued over lunch, and everyone left both filled and fulfilled.

It occurred to me that, after all of that searching, what was missing in my life had found me. I knew that when you're given a lot, a lot is expected in return. By the same token, when you give a lot, you get back more than you ever expected. In essence, you really end up paying it forward to yourself. I was able to add one more thing to my checklist:

- Giving Back (check)

DESTINATION: JOHANNESBURG

"Heyi! Mgnani!"

"Sawubona! Good morning, my friend."

Thandie Masondo and I embraced warmly in the lobby of the Black Diamond Marketing Communications Agency. Thandie had started Black Diamond at 26 years old, just a few years after graduating from business school. She had parlayed her commerce degree into a successful agency specializing in advertising and marketing to young, up-and-coming black professionals in the South African market, the "Black Diamonds" of her generation. Her strategic campaigns were highly sought after by established South African corporations. Thandie and I brainstormed regularly on behalf of a mutual client, a large home goods/decorative accessories retailer.

"You've been a stranger far too long," she said.

"Joburg isn't exactly next door."

"Paf, Canada. I don't understand how anyone could live in such a cold place. You have winter nine months a year. Come home to Africa."

"Are you offering me a job?"

"Are you interested?"

"Don't tempt me."

I felt like one of those clumsy comedic actresses bobbling briefcase, poster tube and sample kit as I followed the long, lithe Thandie down the hall to the boardroom. Her regal Zulu bearing was enhanced by a royal purple charmeuse safari dress. Her smile was blinding and infectious.

"Tea?"

"Rooibos, please."

Thandie poured us each a cup in jewel-colored, cubist-shaped mugs. We had chosen the colors a year earlier. A chrome teapot with a multicolored lid sat canted at an angle like it was about to pour itself. It was funky and fun. The set was from our client's new fall collection.

I unrolled a large world map from the tube and taped it to the whiteboard angled off to the side of the boardroom table. Several countries were outlined in bright colored magic markers, making them stand out against the pale blue ocean background.

"I haven't seen you look this good in ages. Don't tell me you've finally settled down and found someone?" she asked.

"Internet dating was fun for the first couple of years, but I thought I'd never meet anyone. Then I met this man through a mutual friend at a trade show. Go figure, a simple introduction was all it took. I fly to London from here to meet him for the weekend."

"He lives in London?"

"No, Sweden."

"Sweden? Whatever happened to the boy next door?"

"He moved."

Bobby Naidoo, art director for the account, tapped on the door and pushed it open. Bobby was slender, with large brown eyes and the longest eyelashes I have ever seen on anyone. His skin was the color of caramel. He looked cool and elegant in a white polo shirt and crisp jeans. He stopped in front of the map. "I thought this was a presentation on color."

"Howzit, Bobby?" We shook hands. "Yes, it's a presentation on color, the geography of color, past and present. We have to take a look at where we're at so we know where we're going."

"Where are Barbara and Kabelo?" Thandie asked.

Barbara, the media buyer, and Kabelo, the copywriter, had worked for the company since its creation. It was a young team but a seasoned one. Although I was 20 years their senior they treated me like a contemporary, albeit one with experience.

"They're coming just now," Bobby said.

I shook my head at the phrase. As a regular visitor to South Africa I had learned that "just now" could mean anywhere from immediately to three weeks. I hoped it was the former.

Once the group settled in I took them on a tour of color trends across time and place. "Travel is the key to today's trend presentation," I started. "When we travel, we experience a place and we bring the color back with us. We decorate our space, our homes and even our inner selves with the colors of our memories and our experiences. What color is a memory?

"You can draw two lines, one on the map and a timeline that corresponds with it." It started with the early 1990s, when tourists returned from Provence in France and brought back with them the combination of sunflower yellow and Van Gogh's china blue. The colors of Provence were all the rage for at least two years.

I then drew a line from France to Italy. "Who can forget the terra cotta and rustic teal color combination of Tuscany?"

"A color scheme that is still popular in South Africa today," Thandie added.

I drew a line farther south to Greece and flashed a photo of the sundrenched island of Mykonos. "This palette gave us the color name Mykonos Blue, and for a long time patio accessories were blue, white and, of course, brilliant bougainvillea fuchsia."

My world tour took us to more exotic spots with still more exotic color palettes. "As tourists became more adventurous," I said, "they brought back the arts and crafts of the Middle East, whether they were lattice lanterns and mosaic tables from Morocco or decorative tiles and intricate leather work from Tunisia. The spice-inspired colors from the souk permeated homes in the late 1990s."

The dawn of the millennium saw a pared-down look with Scandinavian-inspired designs of distressed woods and weathered pastels. Early in the first decade of the 21st century, we craved the security of home and for a few years we focused on our own local colors. Africa was never more African, and America was all about Americana. But once things stabilized we saw a culture creep.

Retail chains everywhere started showing accessories from far-flung places like Africa, Thailand, India and China. "Fast-forward to the upcoming Beijing Olympics and we will see colors like persimmon and empress yellow taking center stage," I predicted.

"Life is about seeing the local color and appreciating it, reveling in it...trying it on for size. Color trends, just like the places they come from, are a lot like clothes. Some fit better than others. So you try on a color and see how it feels. If you don't like it, you can change it."

I paused for a few minutes for my ideas to sink in. Pens scribbled furiously. Bobby tore sheets of paper from his drawing pad; conversations overlapped. It was fascinating to observe the give and take of ideas, the creative process in action. Joy when ideas worked out, disappointment when they didn't and determination to try again.

Life was like that for me: a crucible for my own creative process, my own experiences. I rejoiced when things worked out and wept when they didn't, but I always kept on trying. I had decided to live a full spectrum of colorful experiences.

It was the perfect metaphor. Some colors, like some experiences, I liked more than others, but I only realized that once I had applied them to the canvas of my life. Just like Bobby, sometimes I had to tear sheets from my own personal drawing pad and start again and again.

Part Four: Exotic Colors

CHAPTER 21:
SWEDISH LESSONS

Vulnerability is all we have, dear Cat. It's what we display every time we meet, touch, hug, kiss and make love. —Lars

My life was complete. I was in a relationship with someone I loved: myself. I enjoyed uncomplicated sex on a regular basis, a fulfilling vocation, an interesting job and a busy social life. I was feeling pretty self-satisfied and confident, except for one thing: I had the right attitude but the wrong approach. I approached life as if it were a series of singular tasks on some to-do list that I checked off once they were done. But it's not just about the pieces; it's about what they add up to that matters—an integrated and whole life. What I learned was that as long as I'm alive, I'm never really done. There's always more to add.

As a student of many disciplines I have become skilled at lots of things like working a room or adapting to any social situation. That is the benefit of a career in sales. The longer I do it the easier it gets to meet and talk to people. The flip side of that is rejection.

On a professional level I learned not to take rejection personally. I know that in business when a buyer doesn't need my product it has nothing to do with me. On a private level, though, when it comes to me and not what I am selling, it is a different story.

I decided to go to the NEOCON design exposition for commercial interiors in Chicago, and I asked Father Goose to come with me.

"You know I can't leave the kids," he said.

"Aren't you being a little overprotective? It's only for the weekend. Marco's almost 18 for goodness sake, and Marissa's 16. Think of it: four nights and three days, drinks at the Sears Tower, dinner at a nice restaurant and breakfast in bed."

"You'll be busy with the conference and clients. "

"There's lots of free time."

"I can't leave them alone."

"Can't or won't? What about your ex?" He rolled his eyes. "Your mom?"

"We're not exactly talking at this moment. No, I can't, it's impossible. It's just bad timing. I'm sorry."

"So am I."

I threw his jeans at him, put on my robe and sat at the edge of the bed feeling a bit put out—okay, rejected. If Father Goose was rejecting the weekend getaway then by extension he was also rejecting me. I let myself take it personally when I knew that 1) ours really wasn't the kind of relationship that included any activities beyond the confines of my apartment, and 2) he doted on his kids. It wasn't as if he was going away with someone else, he really was chief, cook, and bottle washer of his castle.

I was disappointed that Father Goose couldn't or wouldn't make it. But the care and maintenance of his kids (with no backup) meant he was always on call. We managed to see each other in between his trips to the hockey arena, downtown clubs and the local suburban train station. In the end, however, what turned out to be bad timing for Father Goose was a good time for me.

I attended NEOCON by myself. Most of the attendees were earnest young sales reps just out of college. Knowing that, I resigned myself to a quiet weekend in Chicago. As a veteran of these shows I had less than zero expectations.

There was one bright spot and that was the "by invitation only" cocktail/dinner parties thrown by the furniture manufacturers. It was there that I met up with a small group of people who fell outside the above-mentioned category. This group included a long-time friend and colleague, a Danish industrial designer named Nels. Nels was inquisitive, cultured and extremely well read; we had connected instantly. We liked and respected one another. We found in each other many attractive qualities and we would have possibly enjoyed these weekends even more if I hadn't been married for most of the time I knew him. Our ten-year friendship had managed to thrive despite our infrequent meetings. We celebrated our successes in good times and supported each other through bad.

Nels and I caught up in the hotel bar over a drink prior to the opening reception. "I just don't get it," he said, shaking his head in disbelief. "How is it that someone like you is still available?"

"Sometimes I think my love life falls somewhere between Gershwin's 'But Not for Me' and Cole Porter's 'It Was Just One of Those Things.'"

"I don't buy that."

"When it comes to men, I'm done."

"As you wish, but remember, it's the things you don't do that you always end up regretting."

"I'll keep that in mind."

"*Skål,*" we said together as we clinked glasses.

A few hours later Nels introduced me to his friend Lars, a high-profile architect from Stockholm. Lars seemed to me an imposing and unapproachable figure. Perhaps it was his height, or maybe it was the clothes. He was dressed all in black, from his stylish retro Buddy Holly glasses to his cashmere blazer with matching turtleneck and Italian kid leather loafers. He looked like a poster boy for J. Lindeberg.

We chatted politely over cocktails and ended up sharing a table during dinner. I sat next to Nels and continued our conversation. As I glanced across the table at Lars, I thought, too bad he's not my type. He was blond, blue-eyed and fair-skinned, whereas I usually preferred somewhat darker men. I was so looking forward to a weekend of sex and room service.

Nels was always good at reading my mind. "You know," he leaned in and whispered, "he's actually a lot of fun once you get to know him." To which I innocently replied, "Why Nels, whatever do you mean?" We laughed at the shared joke.

The music started and Nels and I hit the dance floor with the first song. It was an R&B orchestra with three vocalists, and they were fantastic. Three or four dances later we rejoined our table, but before I could catch my breath I found myself back on the dance floor, this time with Lars.

He had the grace of a panther. As the tempo changed and the music slowed to a ballad I barely noticed his hand between my shoulders as he pulled me into his arms. Even with heels, I barely came up to his chin.

I tipped my head back and looked him in the eye. His lips hovered lightly above mine for a split second and then he pulled back as he waltzed me in a circle in time with the music. I reminded myself to breathe. I hadn't expected this.

Later over drinks in the deserted hotel bar, I learned more about him. He was quite up-front, as only Swedes can be, about his personal situation. I asked him if he was married.

"Yes."

His candor caught me by surprise.

"But we each have very different lives. We stay together for the sake of our daughter, but soon she'll be in university."

He said he constantly found himself on the road filling in the gaps of his personal life with professional activities. When he was home, which wasn't often, he resigned himself to the three Gs: golf, gardening and gourmet cooking. At 53, he had reconciled himself to a quieter, different kind of life.

"I never expected you," he said, suddenly. "A night like this. I haven't felt this way in a long time."

"You don't have to sell me. I make my own decisions."

"And what have you decided?"

"That I'd already planned to spend this weekend with a lover, except I didn't know it would be you."

I'd like to blame the wine for what happened next, but I hadn't drunk all that much. So I'll blame it on the kiss. It happened so unexpectedly it caught us both by surprise, as did so many things that weekend, including this: when we went to bed that night, nothing happened. Exhausted from all the dancing, we fell asleep.

I have a mental photo album of the places we visited and the things we did. Sometimes I dust it off, page through it and smile in spite of myself. Those early June days in Chicago loom large in my memory as the place where it all began. Dancing, dinner, late-night blues clubs, holding hands and stealing kisses—and our colleagues were none the wiser, except Nels of course.

That weekend may have been cold, wet and grey, but Monday dawned clear and bright. When I pulled back the curtains the sun was shining brilliantly over Navy Pier, and Lake Michigan sparkled. The simple food and easy conversation we shared that morning made it the best breakfast I ever had with a man. I also savored it because I thought it was going to be our last and that we would go on with our lives from there.

It wasn't until the next day, after we'd moved on to our respective next destinations, that we realized we would see each other again. Luckily we both had the kind of careers that enabled us to travel; luckier still, we were able to combine that travel with the opportunity to see one another on a regular basis.

The details of that first weekend are still fresh in my mind. They were preserved by Lars in a deluge of e-mails he sent a few days after the show.

Sweetheart,

Vulnerability is all we have, dear Cat. It's what we display every time we meet, touch, hug, kiss and make love. Without this it's only a good time, casual sex (good but still just sex). Vulnerability and the person behind are all I can offer. But with this come also strength and experience in all aspects... I hope.

Please write again soon. With vulnerable love—Lars

Dear Cat,

I felt last weekend that we ended up in bed very quickly, and maybe too quickly. I believe we both were a little taken by surprise how we both acted. Don't misunderstand me, I loved every second of it and I would have loved to continue and continue and con . . .

Good morning again,

You and me... I'm living in the moment very much now. Did not expect or "plan" for anything like this to happen in my life. I actually started more and more to look at my future in some different aspects and found that maybe I would settle for "what I had" and start to focus on other things besides my marriage. But since two weeks I now have a little other perspective on my life "kind of" and on my thoughts and plans.

Montreal

We walked quietly through the old neighborhoods and admired the architecture, the ubiquitous wrought-iron stairways that spiraled up the front of old grey stone homes. Fuchsia petunias cascaded out of the baskets that hung from lampposts and balconies. We enjoyed each other's company. Conversation came easily and naturally. When we talked, I caught a glimpse of the boy and the man he became, the culture that formed him and continues to shape him, although I'm sure he'd vigorously deny it. I can't say I am a definitive authority on Swedish culture but I did learn a little something about it through Lars.

We came back to my apartment to enjoy lunch on my balcony facing the canal.

"You travel light; I'll say that much for you," he said.

"I keep meaning to buy end tables and some frames for the walls."

"I have two houses of furniture in storage. I'm afraid I'm a bit of a pack rat, but I hate to part with things. I collect furniture by Starck, Wright and Mies."

I recognized the famous designer and architects. I told myself it was only natural he should have an interest in those things. He was an architect, after all. Still, I couldn't help but feel that he found me lacking when it came to what he called "finer nesting instincts."

Lars handed me a small box.

"What's this?" I asked as I untied the blue and gold ribbon.

"It's a CD compilation of music, some of it Swedish, some of it in English. They're some of my favorite songs that I wanted to share with you."

"I was kinda hoping for end tables."

I glanced down at the playlist. Many of the songs were from the 1960s and reflected the six-year age difference between us. I mentioned that we'd come of age in different decades.

"We used to call girls born in the 1960s 'babes in the woods.'"

"So you're the big bad wolf, then?"

"Could be."

"I'll keep that in mind."

"Did you know I saw the Beatles in Germany? My older brother, after much begging, finally gave in and took me to a concert. I think I was about 15 years old at the time, and it was fantastic. I always wanted to play the guitar."

"Do you play any instruments?" I asked.

"Violin."

"Why didn't you take up guitar?"

"My father was a classical musician. He was hoping I'd follow in his footsteps."

"Do you still play?"

"Not any more. It never really interested me. I was happy to stop."

A little cloud of melancholy passed overhead. I felt sorry for the teenaged Lars who longed to play the guitar but did his duty and practiced violin instead. I quickly changed the subject and suggested we head out into the beautiful sunny summer day that awaited us.

There are many souvenir shops in Old Montreal filled with all sorts of Canadiana trinkets and tchotchkes, from maple sugar candies and Canadian flags to Inuit soapstone sculptures and handmade First Nations crafts. Lars was particularly drawn to a jacket made by a well-known First Nations artist.

"I loved reading about history as a kid, especially stories about Indians." He picked up a beautiful fringed suede jacket.

"Look at the workmanship," I said, pointing out the bear claws and beads discretely sewn on the sleeves. "Go ahead, try it on."

"Wow."

"It really suits you."

"Can you see me wearing this in Gamla Stan?"

"Yes, I can."

I could see he was tempted.

A sales lady approached. "Since it's summer," she said, "we're clearing this out. You can get it for half-price."

"Thank you. I'll think about it. Maybe we'll come back."

"Go on, get it," I said. "You know you want it. It looks great on you. Who cares what people think?"

He never did buy that jacket.

London

Every nerve ending in my body was on high alert as I waited for Lars at the Millennium Mayfair Hotel. He had called me from Gatwick and it was only a matter of 20 minutes before he would arrive at my door. It was easy to torture myself with anticipation now that I knew he was only minutes away. It was the weeks between meetings that were unbearably hard.

There were so many things that I loved about Lars, not the least of which was his physical presence. He overwhelmed me with his size; I got lost in his body. His smell was intoxicating and his kisses hungry. He had a way of looking at me like I was the only thing that mattered. Lying next to me in bed, he would trace lazy designs along the contours of my body.

"And here," a finger rested lightly on the tip of my breast, "this is the color of wild raspberries."

"That's a dangerous thing to say, Swede. You'll never be able to look at raspberries again and not think of me."

"I'll take my chances." His fingers roamed farther south and rested at the top of my bikini line. "And here, as we say in Sweden, *slipning pennor och klämma ål*."

"And that means?"

"Sharpening pencils and squeezing eels. A very good fit."

"What can I say? I'm a slightly used virgin."

"Dinner?"

"I don't feel like leaving this spot." My hand traced a path slowly down his abdomen. "Room service?"

Bordeaux

Our schedules were such that we managed to have a brief taste of summer and some wonderful wines in Bordeaux. I leaned back into Lars's chest and admired the view of the vineyards stretched out before us. It hadn't rained in a while and the air was hot and dusty.

"How about a bath?" I asked.

There is something decadent and sensuous about taking a bath with a man. Food, music, candles and champagne round out the experience. And you can talk in a bathtub.

"Good idea, Cat," he said, as we faced each other in a large Jacuzzi tub. "How long has it been now?"

"Two months."

"I'm talking about total time spent together."

"I wasn't counting," I said.

"Fourteen days and 15 nights."

"It's not much when you think about it."

"Yet I feel like we've picked up somewhere in the middle of a story, you and I," he said.

"I know what you mean. It's like we started on page 37."

"You're different than any girl I've ever known."

Over dinner that night Lars told me the story of a fellow architect, a young associate at the firm. Sven had taken an assignment in Tokyo and fallen in love with the delicate Masako, a colleague on the project.

They'd worked closely together over a period of several months. When the assignment ended, Sven decided to change his life completely and stay in Tokyo, leaving behind his wife and daughter. It was a big decision and the only person he felt he could talk to was Lars. Lars had listened carefully, and seeing the relationship for what it was, had encouraged Sven to rethink his decision, consider his position in the firm and their close-knit community and return to Stockholm.

"What did he do?"

"He did what he had to do."

Though I didn't know it at the time, Lars was also contemplating what he had to do. John Lennon once said, "Life is what happens to you while you're busy making other plans." I think both Lars and I were smart enough to realize that neither one of us was going to make any drastic changes to our lives. We were content to live in the moment.

Then Lars was diagnosed with cancer. It was prostate cancer, and while the prognosis was good and the options were numerous, they weren't all that obvious. Surgery, watchful waiting and radiation all weighed heavily on his mind. A clean bill of health was the only thing that mattered, and confident of that, he began to focus on other issues like the side effects from the various treatments.

We spoke after every test, scan and consultation. He was gradually narrowing his options and had all but decided on surgery. It would be a long and tedious recovery given his energetic nature. It would mean weeks at home with no physical exertion. I feared more than anything that he would die of boredom, and I told him so.

"I can work from Helsinki. With my job, it's no problem for me to move temporarily. There is regular ferry service from Helsinki to Stockholm," I said.

"We'll see. We're not there yet."

"Keep it in mind?"

"Yes, of course."

It seemed like such an easy solution to our time and distance problem. Unfortunately it was a solution that hit a little too close to home. Just like the First Nations jacket, I wouldn't fit in. Ours was not a relationship he could wear comfortably in the square at Gamla Stan.

New York

In the weeks before we met in New York, his e-mails were the same.

Baby,

So New York is on. I do prefer NY with you but on the other hand I do prefer you... anywhere. I LOVE TO HEAR YOUR VOICE.

"I love you Lars," I said before I hung up the phone.

"Love to you," he replied. It was not his usual goodbye. I ignored the little voice in my head that said, "Danger—change ahead." I chalked it up to his adding a little variety to our conversation.

I was surprised when he told me he was going to put off the surgery and try the watchful waiting approach to see if his PSA numbers would go down. I had thought he was determined to rid himself of the problem once and for all through surgery, but I was relieved as well; the thought of not being there post-op always created a lump in my throat and a tightening in my chest. I accepted this new decision gratefully.

"I think I may do some sailing with Nels in October in the Greek Isles," he said.

"That sounds like a good idea." I was pleased he could take his mind off of his illness.

"And then there's the Chelsea Garden Show in London this spring."

"I was thinking of going to Tuscany for a week," I countered. I didn't like the fact that I was missing from his long-range plans.

"That sounds like fun. Maybe you can take a cooking class."

I waited for him to ask when, to see about mutual schedules and about going together. But there was no further inquiry on his part. There was an upcoming EcoDesign conference in Washington in October that we were planning to attend, but he didn't bring that up either. And I didn't ask.

I didn't understand how things could change so quickly from one week to the next. Love blinded me to the little hints that littered the short road of our affair.

All weekend he found fault with everything around us: the way people dressed, the way they walked, the way they smoked on the streets. Even a poor doorman at an Upper East Side apartment enjoying a late-night cigarette didn't escape his critical eye.

"What kind of person takes a job as doorman?"

I didn't say anything. I was afraid to rock the boat. What I wanted to say was, "The kind of person who doesn't rob banks, the kind of person who has a family to feed, the kind of person who wants to make an honest living. That's who takes a job as a doorman."

I always knew my working-class background was out of sync with his silver-spoon upbringing. Although we both had highly placed friends and acquaintances, it didn't change the fact that my best friend was a travel agent while his was a member of Danish royalty. I suppose I should have considered myself lucky that he didn't lump me in the same category as those "other Americans," the ones he found so repulsive that weekend.

Lars wanted to go to Coney Island that weekend. The lights and sounds coming from the park were glaring and harsh. It was a difficult place to have a conversation and it was a difficult conversation to have.

"I don't know what's wrong, but I feel like you don't want to be here," I started.

"I don't understand," he said.

"I don't mean *here*, Coney Island. I mean here with me. We're not here together this weekend. It's as if you want to be somewhere else."

"What do you mean?"

"I mean, we've walked everywhere and you're always ten steps ahead. It's as if you're trying to get away from me and I'm running to keep up."

"It's Manhattan. You have to move quickly. What's really on your mind?"

"I'd like to know when I'll see you again. I know all about your plans to go sailing, shopping and golfing. What I don't know is about the next time I will see you. I offered Italy but you didn't say anything."

"I was going to suggest it, but with the illness I'm not sure how to plan."

"Really? You were doing pretty well when you were talking about Greece and London."

"What do you want, Cat?"

"I want to be deliberate in your life. I want to be as deliberate as Nels or a trip to the garden show in London."

"What do you mean by deliberate?"

"Deliberate means I want to be on your calendar. I get the feeling that I'm not. There are three kinds of people in life. There are the essential people, like your daughter. Then there are people who are important, like Nels. Finally, there are people who are convenient. I don't want to be convenient, Lars."

If our conversation was sporadic on the weekend it was nonexistent on the subway ride back to Manhattan. That night Lars's heartburn kept us on opposite sides of the bed for the first time ever. The next morning, prior to leaving for the airport, Lars took me in his arms, and for a second I felt like he would never let me go. Yet I felt finality in his embrace and his kiss goodbye.

A week's silence followed before I received a brief e-mail the day before my Washington conference.

Baby,

Sorry I can't make the conference but the restructuring is a mess and I still have a high-grade sinus infection from the Shanghai trip. Say hi to Nels for me.

—Lar

Lars was in such a hurry and was so unconcerned about what he wrote, or how it sounded, that he hadn't even bothered to finish spelling his name. I responded in kind:

Dear Lar,
Best of luck with the restructuring and I hope you feel better soon.
—Cat

It was the last time I heard from him. I found out many months later from Nels that Lars opted for surgery a month after we saw each other in New York. Why didn't he tell me? Perhaps because he knew me well enough to know that I wouldn't have been able to stay away.

Our love affair spanned half a dozen months in as many cities. And while it was exciting at the time, the unforeseen complication was that these cities were still a regular part of my life either personally or professionally. If I wasn't careful, sometimes the memories associated with him had the ability to cast long nostalgic shadows on an otherwise sunny day. At first it was difficult to be in London, Paris, Montreal, New York or a few places in between and not think of him or us. These days, however, when I find myself in some of these cities, I am there by myself. I hardly ever think of him. Sometimes I wonder if I didn't dream the whole thing. I recall a line from *Romeo and Juliet* that sums up our relationship:

I am afeared, being in night,
All this is but a dream,
Too flattering sweet to be substantial.

It was.

CHAPTER 22:
DANCING FOOL

We're fools whether we dance or not, so we might as well dance. —Japanese Proverb

The doctor held up the X-ray and gave me the bad news.

"You broke your collarbone."

Dr. Weimer, the doctor on call at the local clinic that cold November morning, carefully moved my arm and placed it in a sling. At five feet two inches, he came eye to eye with me. He gave me his best "I am not amused" look as I sat on the examining table. He pushed his wire-rimmed glasses a little higher on the bridge of his nose and blinked several times.

"What are you doing biking so late in the season? We had frost again this morning. What were you thinking?"

Not thinking. Doing. Ever since that disastrous August weekend, my last with Lars, I'd thrown myself into a whole host of activities trying to blunt the hurt and confusion. Like I had done before, I took to the bike path in search of answers. I rode 10 miles every day, rain, shine and now sleet. I listened for answers in the wind, but this time nothing came. The wind no longer played with the leaves in the trees. It roared past me like a freight train. I fought it as I rode out of the city and, as if to spite me, it changed direction and I fought it back.

The physical exertion of these rides and the exhaustion afterward were the only things I could feel. After a hot shower I'd throw myself into my work, calling customers day and night. I used the 12-hour time difference with Asia to my advantage to expand my sales. All the while I avoided making personal sales calls in Europe. I couldn't face all those places yet; too many painful reminders of happier days.

I took a systematic approach to wiping all traces of Lars out of my life. I deleted all but the first few of his e-mails from my laptop, burying them deep within my archives. Next I deleted his phone number lest I stumble upon it inadvertently and experience that sharp, sudden pain in my chest where my heart used to be. I shredded our photos—his photos of me and mine of him. Next I did a sweep of the apartment and threw every gift, CD and souvenir he'd given me into a box and carted it off to the Salvation Army.

"It's only been two months. What if you want these someday?" Annie asked as she watched me. She had a worried look on her face.

"You take them then."

"But weren't there any good memories?"

"Yes, one. I will remember not to do this again. That's the only memory I have."

"At least all this cycling agrees with you. You look great. But how do you feel?"

"Feel? I feel fine."

"Fine. Oh yes, I can see that. Only fine people ride when it's freezing outside."

"Tomorrow is my last ride and then I'll switch to something a little less passive-aggressive, like Yoga."

That was exactly what the universe had in store for me the next day. As I made a nice slow turn onto my street, my front tire hit some frosted cobblestones, the bike slid out from underneath me and I landed on my left shoulder.

Dr. Weimer checked my sling one more time. "This will do just fine. Just try and keep it still." He tore a page from his script pad and handed it to me. "Sleeping pills."

"How long before this heals?" I glanced down at my left arm.

"You'll be good to go by Christmas. In the meantime, try and behave yourself."

"Who me?"

I slid one arm into my coat and draped the other side across my shoulder. This was not going to be easy. I thought of all the things for which

I needed two hands, and it was a long list: driving, typing, washing my hair, drying my hair, ironing, carrying groceries. Between me and a few good friends, I told myself, I'll be fine.

For the next two months I was forced to face facts and move on. I finally figured out Lars's leaving had nothing to do with me and everything to do with him. It's not because of what I said or did, or didn't do. It's not because I didn't have the right furniture, family or friends. It was because he'd changed his mind about me and my ego would not allow for that. How could he? After all, wasn't I "different than any girl he'd ever known?"

I quit beating myself up for being taken in by a man I hadn't really known. Getting to know him had been a process of discovery. People can tell you anything but eventually they will show you who they are. On that thought, I stopped being so hard on myself.

I would entertain no false hope. I would be no lady-in-waiting. I asked myself one question, though. If he reappeared magically one day, if there was a Hollywood ending, would I take him back, knowing how he'd acted during those final days? Would any excuse justify his behavior or his lack of honor? The answer was no. He'd shown me who he was and now, with the blinders off, I didn't particularly like who I saw. It's easier to let go of something you don't want to keep.

It was a slow and painful process but with every passing day both my shoulder and my heart hurt less and less. Once I stopped asking why—because there never really is an answer to that—the next question was how. How do I make myself feel better? How do I get beyond this?

Once again the universe delivered. Christmas came and went and with it the snow and the cold, and for one brief sunshiny day in January 2008 it felt like spring. I grabbed my coat and slid both my arms into its sleeves and went for a walk downtown. The streets were crowded as people took advantage of the fine weather to go out for lunch or do a little shopping. With no particular destination, I walked down St. Catherine Street, ogling the new spring collections in the store windows.

I knew most of the stores that lined Canada's most famous shopping street, and I made mental notes of where I would return once the sales started. As I passed the corner of Peel and St. Catherine, I heard Latin music coming from a theretofore unseen doorway. The lightness of the music suited the weather and my mood. I felt like dancing. That's when I noticed the sign for a new dance club in the doorway.

SALSA!

We're fools whether we dance or not, so we might as well dance.—Japanese Proverb

LESSONS MONDAY NIGHT AT 7:00 $1.50

I watched a video monitor of happy couples dancing to a Latin beat. I fell in love. I'd almost forgotten about my long-held desire to dance. After Gabriel and I left Buenos Aires I had put dancing out of my head. Now it was right here in front of me, calling me to come join the dance. *Bailar conmigo*—dance with me.

I signed up that night for both a group and a weekly private lesson. At the age of 48, I had a lot of catching up to do. The group lessons were fun social events that got me out of the house. The private lessons improved my technique. All the dancing got me back in shape after sitting on my ever-growing behind for eight weeks. Between the lessons and the club I danced four or five nights a week. My backside went from the size of Brazil back down to Bolivia.

At first I thought I'd never be able to look at, let alone dance with, my devastatingly handsome Latino instructor, Fernando. I wasn't sure if I could handle being even slightly attracted to someone. I was still feeling a bit vulnerable but I needed to get over it and quick if I wanted to dance—not just with Fernando, but with anyone else who asked.

Born in Peru, Fernando was an exotic mix of Indian, Spanish and Japanese heritage. His thick black hair, soft brown eyes and easy smile put me instantly at ease. Possessing an irreverent sense of humor, he soon had me laughing at myself and at life in general. His philosophy was that "dance is life."

"Go, Cat, take the space. When in doubt go for the extra turn. He'll move for you, and if not, that's his problem," Fernando said as he led me in a double inside turn.

As the lessons progressed, the steps started to feel different; they started to feel right. I felt more confident of my ability to follow Fernando's lead. He made small tweaks that made a big difference in my comfort level, but just to be certain one night, after a particular sequence of moves, I asked, "Is this right?"

"Does it feel right to you?"

"Yes. I could definitely feel a difference."

"Then it's right," he said. Then he laughed. "Never ask a man his opinion. He'll never tell you the truth. If you ask him if something looks good, he will always say yes. It's about how you feel and not about how someone else makes you feel."

As naive as it sounds, this came as such a revelation that I actually asked Fernando if we could stop so I could write that piece of wisdom down before I forgot it. He laughed, put his arm around my shoulders and gave them an affectionate squeeze. "But you already knew that!" he said.

"Yes," I said.

"Is everything okay, Cat? Even when I see your beautiful smile, you sometimes seem to me—" he paused, choosing his words carefully "—maybe just a little sad."

I felt myself starting to tear up at his kindness and his keen sense of observation. It wasn't very often that Lars invaded my thoughts but he still did on occasion and that day happened to be one of those days. Fernando hit the play button and a Héctor Lavoe salsa mix came up on the speakers. He grabbed my hand and spun me around three times. That made me laugh.

"But not as sad as last week," he said as he dipped me.

I continued to dance, whittling away my waist and tightening up my wobbly bits, but the biggest bonus was the high I felt every time I left the club. The uptick of endorphins and enhanced serotonin levels gave me the same feelings I had when I was with a man, but without the orgasm. Since that's never guaranteed anyway, this felt just as good. I'd traded in sex for salsa and was the happier for it.

"There's a DanceSport Canada Pro-Am Competition. Would you like to enter it with me?" Fernando asked one spring day.

"No."

I paused, realizing how abrupt my answer sounded. "I mean, I'm not a competitive dancer. Not like those other girls. I have to work for every step."

"But right now you're just playing at it. This will help you improve your dancing. We'll enter at the beginner level since you've been dancing for only three months."

"I'm afraid I'll look ridiculous. Silly."

"We're fools whether we dance or not."

"So we might as well dance," I finished the sentence for him.

"*Bailar conmigo*?"

"I'll think about it."

Fernando caught me just as I was about to leave the club. He held out the DanceSport registration. "Fill this out and bring it with you for your next lesson and we'll talk about a rehearsal schedule."

He pushed the form toward me and smiled. I took it and put it in my purse. "Okay."

"Cat? I just want to tell you one more thing before you go. It might help," he said.

I paused in the doorway.

"We're also fools whether we love or not."

CHAPTER 23:
LOVE ITALIAN STYLE

I like you, Red. —Luca

In the Persian fairy tale *The Three Princes of Serendip*, the heroes of the story wander about the countryside finding all sorts of wonderful things they weren't looking for. It was the writer Hugh Walpole who coined the word serendipity for just such occurrences. I have stumbled over many such moments in my life, the most recent of which led to a brief interlude in Trieste and this femoir.

Some chance remarks to several people had a cascading effect that led to circumstances so perfect, I couldn't have planned them. Since I live in Montreal, one of the most beautiful cities in the world, I thought I would be a good candidate for a home exchange in an equally exciting city: London, Paris, Buenos Aires or Prague. Wouldn't it be great to experience a place as a local?

Maugham's quote, "There are too many tourists and not enough travelers," became my lifelong mantra. I wanted more than hit-and-run business trips; I wanted to be a traveler and I didn't want to wait till I retired or won the lottery. I asked for some time off and got it.

I blame it on the postscript, a simple comment appended to a casual e-mail to a friend, an acquaintance really, that yielded a surprising and generous offer. Luca, a retired America's Cup sailor who designs racing boats for love and high-end luxury yachts for money, keeps a pied-à-terre in Trieste to be near his workshop and the highly skilled sailmakers of Monfalcone, but spends the majority of his time on the open water delivering his creations to wealthy customers. As his place was empty most of the year, it was mine for however long I wanted it.

When did I want to pick up the key? he asked. He would be back in the city in May and then again in October for the Barcolana, the big sailing regatta. As this was only February and the idea was really new, I opted for the October date so I could better prepare.

I was able to preview my life in Trieste when a business trip unexpectedly brought me to nearby Munich in early September. Luca, in town a month early, suggested I spend the weekend in Trieste to get a feel for the city and to have a look at the apartment to see if it was suitable.

Luca and I had met eight years earlier at the Montreal Boat Show. I loved to sail, and Gabriel and I had always attended the boat show, hoping someday to buy a new sailboat. Luca and I hit it off instantly, and we stayed in touch, albeit a bit sporadically over the years. It was always easy to pick up where we left off no matter how much time passed.

Luca, Luca, Luca. He was the one bright spot in my lonely married life. How often had I fantasized about spending time with him, discussing books, sailing, having sex? Unbeknownst to him, he was a life preserver used by a drowning woman. Now I wasn't drowning and I wasn't married.

The thought of seeing him again made me a bit nervous, so I pushed it aside. Our relationship up to this point had been one of friendly acquaintances and nothing more. Luca's e-mails were always polite and to the point.

Everything changed the moment he saw me coming through the arrivals door at Ronchi Airport. He didn't recognize me. I'd changed a great deal over the past eight years. I'd blossomed since my divorce. I was more confident. I had grown my hair, bought new clothes and perfected my curves through dancing. Most important, I was back to being happy. Whatever it was, Luca was surprised.

Three times on the drive into the city, he complimented me on my looks. I thanked him, but chalked up the kind words to pleasant surprise on his part and proceeded to ignore them. After all, I thought, he is Italian. As I studied his profile I could see he hadn't changed at all. He was unusually tall for an Italian at six feet three inches, a trait he attributed to an Austrian ancestor on his mother's side. His dark curly hair fell to his shoulders. He wore it in a short ponytail. Perpetually tanned from life on the water, his swarthy coloring accentuated his green eyes and broad smile. Throw in a gold earring and he looked like a modern-day Sinbad waiting to ravish the next beauty.

Throughout the weekend we walked around the city, stopped for gelato at Zampoli's, drank coffee at Willy's and dined along the canal. During that time I got to know both Trieste and Luca a bit better. We talked about relationships in general and some of Luca's in particular.

"Italian women are tough," he groaned.

"All Italian women, or only the ones who know you?"

Luca laughed. "It's a small city."

"What usually happens in my case is I become friends with the guy and before you know it we're past the point of no return for a relationship. We're in the friend zone," I said.

"This I know."

We passed the afternoon in companionable silence as if we'd known each other for years. Just friends. I didn't say anything but I thought that's exactly where we were at that moment. I couldn't figure out if I was disappointed or relieved.

Luca made me dinner our first night in the city. It was his special gorgonzola lasagna. It was perfect, except for one thing: he forgot to add the key ingredient, the gorgonzola.

"Stop it," he smiled.

"Stop what?"

"Stop distracting me." Then he made me promise never to tell anyone about his mishap in the kitchen. "I have a reputation to maintain, you know," he said.

"It'll cost you."

"I'm willing to pay. Are you?"

Was I? I was scared and excited at the prospect.

When we weren't walking we were touring the countryside on his Ducati motorcycle. Normally motorcycles scared me. Gabriel had a motorcycle, and when I rode with him I always felt exposed and vulnerable. I didn't trust his ability to handle the bike or me. But I trusted Luca. I never once felt afraid; in fact I wanted to go faster and I never wanted to get off. I liked the feel of my arms around his waist and my chest pressed against his back, and he did too. But neither of us said anything.

One night we rode the motorcycle to a small restaurant tucked away into the hills surrounding Trieste. We dined al fresco on the specialties of the house: a Triestine gnocchi and veal dish. Our usual polite but friendly conversation continued as we discussed the many things we had in common and a few things we didn't.

We were both avid readers, so I was surprised to learn that Luca hated poetry. He said it was because they were forced to memorize Dante in school. He recited a line to prove it.

"Perchč mi schianti? Perchč mi scempi? Non hai tu spirito di pietade alcuno? Uomini fummo ed ora siamo fatti sterpi . . ." (Why do you pierce me, why do you hurt me? Have you no spirit of pity? Once we were men now we are trees.)

The quote caught me off guard. For some reason it made me think of Lars, and that brought tears to my eyes. It had been a year and I couldn't believe he still affected me. Suddenly I felt quite vulnerable when I had no reason to. I was sitting across the table from a very attractive man who, apart from a few compliments, had no interest in me. It was safe. I was safe.

"What's wrong?" he asked.

"Cigarette smoke," I said, making a waving motion with my hand.

After dinner we took a ride to a lookout near the little town of Santa Croce. We bent the rules a bit and took the bike to the very top of the hill. It was a clear night with a full moon. It was as if someone had shone a spotlight on the bay.

"Do you have a nickname?" He looked at me expectantly.

"It's Red."

"Red. I like you, Red." He tugged on my hair like some shy adolescent.

"I like you too. But then I've always liked you."

"No, I mean it." He bent down and kissed me softly on the lips. "I like you," he repeated, and he kissed me again in just the same way. It was my turn to be surprised.

How quickly the image of Lars receded and was replaced suddenly by Luca. Was that all it took? I wondered. In a flash, the old feelings and longings were replaced by the new. It was as if Lars had never existed.

How fickle we are. In Shakespeare's *Much Ado About Nothing,* Benedick puts it best when he says, "For man is a giddy thing and this is my conclusion." Even in those first few hours, as romance blossomed, I couldn't help but wonder who would replace Luca in my affections once this tryst ran its course. And I knew it would run its course. Luca was a sailor in the literal and metaphorical sense of the word.

The trouble is that love is blind. I was so happy with the way things turned out that weekend, I could have flown home without the plane. Trieste was definitely a go.

Reality quickly set in once I returned home and started to pack. Given his history and capricious nature, I thought Luca's interest in me would dissipate after our brief weekend together. I wasn't expecting him to stay in touch or call as often as he did. But he kept up the connection either through Skype or e-mail.

Luca a scritto: Eh Red, I really miss you. You coming out from the airport arrival with your big black bag and your deep green eyes. I can buy you an ice cream factory tonight.

I responded in kind. In a digital world where memories get erased with a keystroke, I responded the old-fashioned way. I sent some cute greeting cards to a very real but empty mailbox. It was the first romantic gesture on my part, and it wasn't lost on him. The next gesture was his. He called on Tuesday to find out what my plans were for the weekend. If I wasn't busy, could he come for a quick visit?

"To Montreal?"

"That's where you are, right?"

I'd just left him a week earlier and now I was astonished and delighted by his proactive approach. He didn't have to ask twice. I began to make plans for the weekend.

It's funny, but the heart-pounding, nerve-tingling anticipation I'd felt with Lars didn't happen with Luca. I felt more or less detached from the coming weekend, probably because I suspected our next encounter would be our last. Our lives were totally different and it would be years, if ever, before our paths would cross again. This was a temporary, enjoy-the-moment fling. In three weeks' time I would go to Trieste and I would pick up a key. He would sail off into the sunset and we would be history. I'd be on my own to enjoy life in Italy in general and in Trieste in particular. *Facile, facile*, as the Italians like to say.

The weekend in Montreal was a continuation of the one in Trieste. It was a weekend of exploration, first of the city and then of each other. I introduced him to a few friends, who found him charming and funny. During brunch on Sunday Annie pulled me aside.

"So what do you think?" I asked.

"As someone who has been a spectator to your love life over the last few years, I am telling you now, Cat: *be careful.*"

"What do you mean?"

"I see how you look at him. It's not the same for him."

"I know that," I said. "C'mon. What do you think of him, really?"

"Okay, I like him better than Lars. He's much more approachable. And he seems more reliable than Adrio."

"But?"

"Cat, he's not the first man to cross an ocean or a continent for you. And he won't be the last. Remember that guy from L.A.? And what about the one from Calgary? This is an entirely new species. I call them the experiencers. They don't even stay around long enough to be bad boys."

"Don't worry," I told her.

"I won't worry if you promise you won't get attached."

"Deal."

"Cat?"

"Yeah?"

"Leave the red suitcase at home. This is not that kind of move, no matter what you think."

I was all set to make good on my promise to Annie, but there was a complication. Luca would not be leaving Trieste as anticipated; he would have to stay an extra three weeks while his team readied a boat for delivery to a customer in the Caribbean. He offered me the choice of arriving while he was still there and spending time with him, or arriving later in the month just before he was to leave.

I wanted to spend the time with Luca, however little it would be. It was the first time in four years that I'd lived with a man on a daily basis, if only for a few weeks. Because we knew the time was limited we didn't waste a minute of it.

Luca showed me a Trieste I would never have known had I just followed the guidebooks. He showed me places that were significant in his life. He told me his stories and I learned a lot about him.

"This is my high school. My father wanted me to go to university, but it wasn't for me."

"What did you do?"

"I did what every rebellious boy does. I ran away and found work, a little here, a little there. I traveled and I attended college in the US."

"So that explains why you speak such good English. And your dad?"

"He took it out on my little sister. She wanted to go to art school but she earned a PhD in particle physics instead. He's very proud of her. Me, I'm just a boat builder. We never spoke much after that. It's ironic because my father was a sailor who only wanted his freedom. And then he met my mother and before long they had a family. We were an anchor, not one that secured his mooring but one that prevented him from going. I have the life he wanted for himself."

I kept my stories to myself—it's a lot easier to give your body away than your soul—and left Luca to guess at the woman he thought was me.

"You're a perfectionist, Red, I can tell. You shouldn't expect too much from me," he said one day.

"I don't expect anything from you other than you be honest with me. My world is populated by imperfect people who work on perfecting themselves every day. That's what makes them my friends."

"And you think too much."

"Hey, what happened to my beautiful green eyes?"

To tell the truth, when it comes to thinking too much or not thinking at all, I prefer the former. It keeps people from taking advantage of me. It keeps me from being indiscriminant and accepting just anything. That whole nonsense about just letting go and being in the moment is so passé, so 1980s. Some people, though, get stuck in a generation and never leave.

For three weeks we combined a schedule of work and play, Italian style. Every day we ate lunch and dinner together, either at home or in a neighborhood restaurant. Evenings were spent talking about current affairs, books, cultures—his and mine—or politics. Afterward we strolled around the city hand in hand.

At night we made love with a sense of urgency driven by a circle on a calendar. Each day was another day gone. Each time I could feel myself falling off the cliff into a sea of nothingness, into a state of suspended animation that lasted a heartbeat before I broke the surface gasping for breath. Everything became an act of love, from him washing my hair to feeding me chocolate between kisses while we watched movies on the couch.

Weekends were filled with road trips to neighboring towns and villages. We returned to Santa Croce, this time during the day to watch the Barcolana regatta. We sat hidden in the grass, far from the crowd. Feeling a bit daring I peeled off my top. Luca was an expert with bras. I didn't even feel his touch as it came undone.

The following weekend we took the train to Venice. He surprised me with two first-class tickets early one Sunday morning. We arrived in time for a lunch of fresh pasta with squid ink. The things I tried for that man. He kissed me on every bridge in Venice.

"I'm very happy," he said, as we sat in the Piazza San Marco eating ice cream.

"So am I," I replied, but somehow I knew I'd never be this happy again. I knew that in a week's time I would have to let him go. He was free and his was a lifestyle that could never be adjusted, and I knew that. I had to accept and adjust myself.

As if reading my mind, he leaned in and said, "Red, I'm glad we're friends."

"Me too." At least we'll always have that, I thought. It's where we started and it's where we would end.

In our final week together Luca introduced me to several of his friends whom I could contact if I needed anything during my stay. As if to ensure I knew exactly where we stood, he began systematically to position himself for his departure and head off any possible requests I might have. I had none and was quite surprised by this, because I'd never asked him for anything and never would. I felt hurt, but I reasoned that this was his way of casting off an anchor and setting sail forever free.

"I'm not interested in getting married," he said one day.

"Okay," I replied. A 20-year marriage veteran, I had no intention of re-enlisting. I thought it was presumptuous that he would even think I wanted to marry him.

It was during our last lunch together that he made his declaration of independence. He reminded me he was free and he added for good measure that emotions were dangerous things. “I spent a long time training myself not to have any,” he added.

I struggled to control my own. Luca certainly had his lines down pat when it came to women and parting scenes. I saw the play unfolding before me. I knew the end, yet I hoped that maybe, somehow, I was different.

The next day, his bags packed and taxi waiting, we said goodbye. Compared to what we’d shared the past three weeks, it was a bit anticlimactic. I felt serene and was ready, even eager, for my next adventure once he walked out that door. I’d prepared myself well, so the goodbye went easier than I thought it would.

What I wasn’t prepared for were the daily text messages, phone calls and e-mails that followed his departure. Perhaps those three weeks had meant more than either of us thought. Why bother to stay in touch otherwise? I was surprised by his efforts and I returned them in kind.

Life was good. I used Luca’s place as a pied-à-terre and traveled extensively in Europe. Just when I thought things couldn’t get any better, Luca announced a return trip to Trieste to finalize some business before flying to Sydney to work on a new boat concept with an Australian firm. I was thrilled; I’d be able to take advantage of a few weeks of good suppers, good sex and good conversation one last time before returning home to Montreal. It would be a great way to finish off my stay in Italy. I would come full circle.

I like neat and tidy endings, things that are predictable. For once things would end as expected. I tried not to notice the change in tone and tenor coming from Luca as his messages became fewer and more like co-ordinates on a ship’s chart. I blissfully assumed nothing had changed. In hindsight I can almost hear when the click of disconnection happened. It was a few weeks after his initial departure, when we were communicating almost daily. I wrote an e-mail that summarized our three weeks together. It was a way for me to hang on to those moments, to keep a record to prove that they had actually happened. For Luca it was a love letter he could never respond to. It showed him we were no longer on the same page.

Dear Red,

Hope you are having a good time in Italy. Here I'm very busy these days with lots of activities as we get ready to make our final run to St. Kitts. My schedule is already filled for the next weeks and every day should have 48 hours to have everything done. I hope mid December things will slow down a little.

I wanted to let you know that I received your DOC and I never received anything like that… My only consideration is that you have been very nice in describing Dr. Jekyll, but what about Mr. Hyde? Better not thinking about him?

I think it's healthy to have a good dose of skepticism. Life, people, ideas etc. cannot be so nice/perfect after all. Even the pope goes to the bathroom every day.

Anyway I thank you for the beautiful love letter, for me it is a "love letter" anyway… As I told you I have never received anything like this, and my ego is as large as the Kilimanjaro at its base in Moshi.

It's bad that it comes as a computer file, it's electronic vapor. A handwritten copy will be something I will keep forever. Something I can read once in a while thinking about how I could have been if I was a real good person. Something I can blackmail you with for the rest of your life.

On my side I have to recognize my limits and tell you I will never be able to write something like this. I like your Hyde parts too much. I always preferred the inferno in Dante's Divine Comedy. *Beatrice is not my kind of girl.*

One day I will show you, slowly-slowly, my worst parts. Some can be fun.

In the meantime I can only send you the biggest and most tender kiss you have ever received.

Thanks, Luca

It was the polite closing of "thanks" that gave it away. But once again I glossed over that fact in favor of fantasy. I was more than willing to have him blackmail me for the rest of my life. I also looked forward to seeing some of his worst parts. For me it meant there was a future if only for a few weeks in January.

His request for a hard copy gave me an idea. I planned to leave a handwritten copy of the letter in his apartment where he would stumble upon it the next time he was in town. I bought some fine Italian stationery and brought it back to the apartment, but the letter, my words, would never find a home on paper.

CHAPTER 24:
CIAO TRISTEZZA

For me, life is like a book. It's one continuous narrative and the best and only thing you can do is be the author of your own adventures or misadventures, as the case may be. —Cat

The New Year arrived and with it a new Luca. This Luca was a stranger to me, and I learned within a few days of his arrival that there was to be no Trieste redux. The tender moments of the past were replaced with chilly politeness. After all, we were still sharing a space.

It was confusing at first, but as I considered Luca's nature, sadly it made sense. The difficult part was him having to show me how things had changed when telling me would have been so much kinder. I was relying on our friendship and those honest conversations we had shared to help get us through things, but I was mistaken.

I knew for certain when I saw the toilet seat up in the bathroom on his first day back. It was the most male of habits, but it had never occurred to me that it was one of his habits because it had never happened before. Putting the toilet seat down was a small courtesy that no longer occurred. The significance of this wasn't lost on me. Neither were the single loads of laundry he was doing or his newfound interest in wearing his bathrobe to sleep when he'd always slept in the nude.

"Are you still comfortable having me in your space?" I asked.

"Yes, of course. You stay as long as you like."

"My return ticket is flexible. I can leave at any time."

"Red, it's fine. You're fine."

In an effort to make myself scarce around the apartment, I took up afternoon residence at the Café Audace. From the moment I first walked in I felt at home. It was a historic café that had been given a new lease on life and a new retro style. With windows that provided a view of the Piazza Unita, the harbor and the surrounding hills, the place inspired me.

Audace. I loved the name, I loved to say it and, more importantly, I loved its meaning. There is a very subtle difference between its meaning in French and Italian and the English definition of the word. Audacious: *Webster's* defines it as a bold or arrogant disregard of normal restraints, while the French and Italian definitions are a bit more understated:

Mouvement de l'âme qui porte à des actions extraordinaires, au mépris des obstacles et des dangers. Être plein d'audace.

Movement of the soul that leads to extraordinary actions in defiance of obstacles and dangers. Be full of daring.

Una persona intrepido coraggioso

An intrepid and courageous person.

It was in the Café Audace that I made my plans for my last few weeks in Trieste. It was in the Café Audace that I poured my heart onto the page because I wouldn't allow myself to cry. All of the emotion I felt went into my writing, and slowly I began to get my bearings.

Dateline: Trieste, Italy—January 2009

In the Hollywood version of The Princess Bride, Westley (the pirate) is resuscitated and brought back to life. He marries Princess Buttercup and they ride off happily into the sunset. Many years ago, when I first read William Goldman's version of the story, he explained that the original ending was meant to be quite different. In the real version of the story, Westley dies and there's nothing to be done.

In his abridgement of this lovely little tale, Goldman learns and passes on a valuable lesson: "Sometimes life is just not fair." As someone who is used to the proverbial happy ending, I should have taken issue with that ending but, at the time, I found some comfort in the fact that someone finally told the truth. And so, like most 21-year-olds, I filed that bit of wisdom away for use at a later date.

A few years later I was walking by a downtown skyscraper when I passed a bag lady holding a sign that read, "$1 for a piece of my mind." As I was, and still am to some extent, in a hurry, I thought the sign said "$1 for peace of mind."

And so I dropped a dollar in her cup and moved on. "Hey girlie, yeah you, Red! Ain't no such thing as a Hollywood ending," the bag lady yelled after me.

That did not give me peace of mind. I knew she was right, but somehow there had to be an exception, at least for me. I had conveniently forgotten William Goldman's adage on life.

I quickly learned that there were no exceptions, no 11th-hour cavalry rescues and no knights in shining armor. The truth is that people die, promotions don't materialize, the castle is drafty and the prince runs off with the scullery maid. In the second act, your job gets outsourced, you gain weight in strategic places, lovers lie and children keep coming home. So much for happily ever after.

Happily Ever After. What does that mean? I think too often we make the mistake of believing that happily ever after is a place, a destination, an endpoint. But it's not. If, as they say, life is a journey, then the best you can hope for are little pit stops of happiness along the way. Are we there yet? We used to ask our parents? No! According to Gertrude Stein, there is no there there.

For me, life is like a book. It's one continuous narrative and the best and only thing you can do is be the author of your own adventures or misadventures, as the case may be. Write your own script, don't let someone else write it for you. Make a decision (any decision); if it's the wrong one, fix it. Do your own "interior" decorating and use all the crayons in the box. Give yourself permission and don't let analysis paralysis rule your life.

I came to this realization a bit late in life. Then again I was always something of a late bloomer. It's only in the last five years, since my divorce, that I've been acquiring a colorful new perspective on life. Sometimes it's fun, other times it's puzzling and many times it's damn hard.

I'd like to think I'm a littler wiser, rather than worse, for the wear and tear on my soul. And by and large I am. The mistakes are fewer, the pleasures simpler and the down times a whole lot shorter than they used to be.

At the end of the day, many of the steps forward you take, you take by yourself. Sometimes you get a little help along the way. That's why God invented your mother, sisters, daughters and girlfriends. (Sometimes I think God should have quit while he was ahead.) And then of course there are those other steps, too... you know, the ones that have you going around in circles or just plain backward. Unfortunately, those steps are yours alone, every single one of them.

The good news is, as a woman you can always stop and ask for directions. That's not an easy thing to do, especially when you're trying to show that you're calm, confident and in control. How can you ask for help when you're trying to live up to a role that you think everyone expects you to fulfill, that of Wonderful Woman?

That is especially true for me. A lot of people (friends, family members and acquaintances) tell me they live vicariously through me. And I must admit that on paper it all looks pretty exciting and maybe even a little glamorous. Sometimes it is, but most of the time it's a lot of work and it's occasionally a little lonely.

I have traveled the world for my job and have lived in a couple of very lovely cities. My name actually sounds like it belongs to a character in a novel (and I guess in a way it does). But things are not always as they appear and that's why I decided to write it all down, to set the record straight for myself. Because sometimes I am in danger of believing my own press, and it's always better to be humble than to be haughty. It's a much shorter fall when things don't work out.

I often think about what Canadian-born actress Marie Dressler once said when she turned 50: "By the time we hit fifty, we have learned our hardest lessons. We have found out that only a few things are really important. We have learned to take life seriously, but never ourselves."

Sometimes when things feel a bit overwhelming, as they do now, I try to take Marie's advice and focus on those things that are really important while not taking myself too seriously. Like Marie, I don't really want or need the drama. I much prefer a good comedy.

And so I'm sitting in my favorite café in the Piazza Unita in Trieste, a lovely little city in Northern Italy. I'm jotting down a few hasty notes during what little time I have left as I reflect on the steps that led me here and those steps I have yet to take. How I got here, well that's an enlightening tale with so many twists and turns that if it didn't really happen to me, it could almost be a novel.

I reflected on the meaning of loss and realized the only man worth crying over was a dead one. That's real loss. Anything else is a blessing.

The next two weeks, while Luca traveled, were mine, free and clear. During that time I said my goodbyes to the places and people I'd come to know in a city I'd grown to love. I lined up side trips to Verona, Florence, Milan and cooking school in Bologna. I would use my time to say goodbye to Italy as well. I doubted I would ever return.

During those last few weeks Luca and I spent only four days occupying the same space. One of those days was the day of Barack Obama's inauguration. Luca has very liberal leanings, so I thought he would be pleased. We were watching history in the making together on television.

"I don't care who Skypes me. I'm not answering. This is a historic moment," I said.

We waited for the introduction of dignitaries and then Obama took the platform. Luca chose that exact moment to make a phone call and carry on a lively conversation with a colleague. He'd had all afternoon to make that call, yet at the precise moment of the speech he'd decided to interrupt the broadcast. I gave him the benefit of the doubt and chose to take the high road. I refused to let it upset me. I put on my headset and logged on to MSNBC and watched the ceremony on my laptop. I took some comfort in the fact that I was leaving the next day for cooking school and we wouldn't have to disturb each other again. Meanwhile, the travel agent was going to get back to me with return flights to Canada.

A few days later I walked into the apartment and startled him. I'd spent a happy three days in Bologna, cooking and eating.

"You look good," he said. It was the same line he'd used the first day I saw him in Ronchi Airport.

"Don't start," I said.

"How was it?"

"Now I know why they call it Bologna the Fat. By the way, I've moved my flight up. I'm leaving next week."

"I understand."

"I knew you would."

Later that night for the first time in weeks, he pulled me into his arms. My head lay on his chest. We stayed there, saying nothing and not moving, for what felt like hours, but it was only a few minutes. Then I returned to my side of the bed. It was confusing after so many weeks of not touching each other. I wanted to kiss him because I knew it would be the last time. But I couldn't. I deserved better and I wouldn't let myself be taken in one last time, nor would I give myself away. Somewhere along the way he may have lost all respect for me, but I still had a deep well of respect for myself.

My return flight home was Saturday, February 14. How appropriate, I thought, to be returning home to something I loved, Montreal, on Valentine's Day.

My final act of defiance was to spend my last night in Trieste in the Hotel Posta. By noon on Friday the 13th, three suitcases stood at attention in Luca's living room. I did a once-over through the apartment and then took my bags to the hotel, returned to the studio and kept myself busy until dinner time and Luca's return.

"What happened to your suitcases?" he asked.

"I moved them to the hotel."

"You what?"

He stared at me, his mouth forming words I couldn't hear. I'd caught him off guard. I'd managed to achieve some balance in the situation. I'd chosen my own exit. He wasn't the only one who was free.

"You didn't have to do that."

I shrugged. It was my turn not to have to explain myself.

"I hate you, I really hate you." His eyes welled up; it was an amazing display of pseudo-emotion. He removed his glasses and rubbed his eyes. Good, I thought, how does it feel? Somehow I wanted to believe this was more than a show for my benefit, but I couldn't.

"How can you hate someone you don't have any feelings for?" I asked.

We ate a quiet dinner. He sat in sullen silence and I slipped into sales mode. I kept the conversation light and amusing, talking about movies and books. It wasn't the first time I had worked to keep up both ends of a conversation. It was a replay of so many of the dinners we'd suffered through over the last several weeks. I'd be damned if I let him affect my evening.

Every so often he would just shake his head in disbelief that I'd changed the endgame to suit me. However friendly he would like to make that last goodbye, I was not going to let him. In the end we were not friends and we would never be again. If I'd learned one thing about Luca, it was that he would never change. He would go on collecting and disregarding women, leaving a trail of broken hearts in his wake.

Luca walked me to the hotel after dinner.

"Thank you for everything," I said. "Trieste is a gift I will always treasure."

"It was nothing. Thank you for the DVD and the backpack. You shouldn't have troubled yourself."

"It was no trouble at all." We stood there for a minute. "Well, goodbye then," I said.

Luca stepped in front of me and wrapped his arms loosely around me. I made a feeble attempt at a hug by raising one arm slightly and patting his back halfheartedly. He kissed the top of my head. It was an embrace I couldn't return.

It could have been, should have been, so much more. The bittersweet ending I'd scripted all those weeks ago had been drastically different than this.

Seven of the top ten of the AFI's (American Film Institute) greatest love stories feature couples who do not end up together. We could have been one of those great love stories; instead, our affair had no more depth or substance than a shared cappuccino at a local coffee bar. What a pity.

Luca stood on the sidewalk and watched me walk through the double doors of the hotel. I could feel his eyes on me, but I didn't look back. I asked for my key and walked up the steps to the elevator. The doors opened and I walked in. I punched the button and turned to face forward only once the doors had closed.

CHAPTER 25:
A CAFÉ GIRL IS BORN

"You're a real woman, with a real job, and you live in the real world." —Mel

I arrived back in Montreal on Valentine's Day 2009. Never mind that I arrived in the middle of a cold snap with temperatures so frigid they nearly froze my Italian leather shoes to the sidewalk. It didn't matter; I was back in the city I loved, and on Valentine's Day. It was my gift to myself. Rather than see irony in the situation as a cynic might, I saw only how right and fitting it was. That's the optimist in me.

More importantly, I fell into the arms of girlfriends who, with very little notice, came to my rescue. We were *Sex and the City North* and I was Carrie Bradshaw, returning from a disastrous Paris experience minus Mr. Big. There was, however, one small glitch: when I left, since I didn't know how long I'd be traveling, I'd given up my apartment. When I returned, not only was I heartbroken, I was homeless. Luckily for me that was no impediment to my resourceful friends.

Zara was waiting at the airport, car warmed and ready to "come pick" me as she likes to say in her charming Syrian accent.

Nadia made a few quick phone calls and found a furnished place for me at a very reasonable rate. It wasn't just any apartment; it was in the heart of the city with a view that took my breath away and my mind off my troubles. Inside were a lovely orchid plant and a bowl of bright red apples to comfort me. Nadia had even made sure the Internet and the satellite TV were activated.

Annie wasn't far behind with a bag full of groceries and some toiletries. It was like I'd never left, like I'd dreamed the whole thing, awoken from a nightmare and found myself in safe and familiar surroundings. Whew, that was a close one!

We celebrated a belated Valentine's Day, just us girls, a few days later at a cozy little restaurant on McGill. Tucked away in the corner we ordered tapas and 'tinis and we toasted ourselves and celebrated our first UnValentine's Day.

"To us," Zara said, raising her glass.

"To us," Annie, Nadia and I chimed in.

"And to Cat, who has come back to us and her favorite city," Annie said.

"Rick and Ilsa may have Paris, but I'll always have Montreal," I said.

"To hopeful romantics," Nadia added.

We clinked glasses, ordered one more round and then bundled up to face the long walk back to our cars. The conversation continued through chattering teeth and puffs of warm breath visible to all once they hit the cold night air.

"Look," Annie said, pointing at the Montreal skyline lit up against an ink-black sky.

Looking at that skyline at night surrounded by my friends, the inner turmoil of the previous weeks subsided for a few minutes. I was at peace, safe at home. I exhaled for the first time in weeks, and it felt good.

"And nnnow what?" Zara asked.

"Get busy, back to work. It's time to go somewhere warm for a change. My MMMMexican colleagues have asked me to come down and make a presentation to a customer. I think maybe a little sunshine will dddddo me good."

"And don't forget ssssalsa," Nadia added.

I sighed.

"What's that sigh?" Annie asked.

"I just don't feel like dddancing."

"But you always dance ssssalsa," Zara said.

"You came in second in the ProAm last year," Nadia reminded me.

No one was more surprised than I was when the judges presented me with a small trophy. I thought of the trophy now, one of the few decorative pieces I owned, sitting somewhere in storage. I'd have to dust if off and give it a prominent place in my new apartment as a reminder of a brilliant comeback. The question was: could I do it again? This time I wasn't so sure.

We said goodbye in the parking lot with our usual Montreal two-cheek kisses.

It was still early by the time I got home to my downtown apartment. The floor-to-ceiling windows provided a great view of surrounding skyscrapers. The skyline inspired me. I sat down at my desk and turned on my laptop. I reread the essay I had written at the Café Audace just three weeks before. It was titled, "Ain't No Such Thing as a Hollywood Ending." Hmmm, it's not the most optimistic title. Who knows, I thought, maybe in a few months time I'll feel differently and change it.

Like Zara said, now what? It was only February. This was going to be a long year. How I yearned for a new decade, a fresh start, a clean slate. The year 2010 couldn't come fast enough.

I opened my e-mail and sent a quick note to my friend Julie in Johannesburg, attaching my essay. I don't know why I sent it to Julie. Perhaps it was because hers was the most recent e-mail in my inbox. And then I went to bed. When I powered up my laptop in the morning and started my work day, my first day back in months, I had over 500 e-mails. And right at the top of the pile was Julie's reply. The subject line read, "Is this a book?"

A book? Who is she kidding? I thought. It's three pages of my heart bleeding all over the page. I sent her a note thanking her for the compliment and telling her that it was just an article I was thinking of submitting to More.com, an on-line women's magazine, once I got through what looked like a month's worth of e-mails.

A book. I couldn't get the idea out of my head. I'd felt better after writing that piece and gaining some insight into where I was at that moment in time. Perhaps writing down my experiences of the past few years would give me the same insight about my life and where it was heading.

When I started dating again after all those years of marriage, I was excited, enthusiastic and optimistic. I was convinced that all I needed to feel complete was a solid partner to share all of the good things in my life. Yet four years later, still alone, I knew that even if I didn't share all my gifts with anyone special, it didn't diminish the value of the gifts. I still had a great family, amazing friends and interests too numerous to keep track of. No. Finding someone to fill a hole was not the answer.

Learning to dance salsa was fun but it was fleeting. And travel, while it was a good diversion, was only a temporary solution. After all those miles, I still came home to me. Volunteering to teach English was also fun and fulfilling—but maybe it was time to become my own teacher.

Looking over the last four years, I no longer saw a desert. I saw a rainforest. It was fecund, wild and colorful. It was full of new experiences from the simple to the sublime. The landscape of my past was populated with exotic flowers, colorful birds, strange insects and wild animals. It changed daily and it was starting to overgrow the boundaries of my memory.

Perhaps if I wrote it all down, if I dusted off my rusty writing skills, I might be able to put together a story that made sense of the past and shed a little light on the present, on who I am, how I got here and what I have learned about myself along the way. Rather than avoid the thought of Luca, perhaps writing about him was a way to face facts in black and white, a way to work through the hurt and disappointment. It certainly would be less painful than breaking a collarbone.

Every day I wrote a few lines, a paragraph or sometimes a page—about as much as I could stand before tears blurred my vision. I was kidding myself if I thought I could outrun those tears. He hijacked my life a second time in absentia; I never knew when I'd feel the slightest bit emotional. I wore dark glasses on airplanes and warned customers of "asthma" attacks that might require me to leave the room immediately. Mentally I knew I had to detach myself and forget about him; emotionally was another story.

I tried pushing him from my mind, but the harder I pushed the longer he stayed. It took me a while to figure out it was okay to think about him for a few minutes and then move on. I had to accept the fact that he was living rent free in my head for the time being, and that while he may have had me, it wouldn't be forever.

As I reread the chapters I wrote about Luca I pretended I was okay. I knew I would keep on pretending until one day I actually felt okay. In the meantime, my friends and family were none the wiser. As for friends in Trieste, all they knew was that I had been called back early to attend to a project in Canada.

April and spring came to Montreal, but I hardly noticed. I was so engrossed in my writing project that I stopped dancing, answering e-mails and accepting social invitations from friends. Every night I moved my laptop from my home office to my kitchen table and wrote a few paragraphs. I would spend entire weekends just writing.

One night, I'd just hit the save button when there was a knock at my door. I opened it to find my friend Giacomo standing in the doorway. Giacomo Morelli, short, bald and with a slight pasta belly, is one of the sexiest men I know.

He peered at me over his Armani frames and did a double take. "*Ma dai,* it's 7:00 p.m. and you're still in your PJs. What have you been doing? Everyone is worried sick about you. No one has seen or heard from you in weeks."

He looked around the kitchen at the hundreds of Post-it notes affixed to the table, shelves, fridge and cupboard doors. These were the notes for my book.

"What the? It looks like a bomb exploded in here."

I struggled with how to explain. Telling friends I was writing a memoir sounded self-indulgent.

He brushed past me and put a bottle of chilled white wine on the kitchen counter. He rummaged through the drawers in search of a corkscrew. He pulled two wine glasses out of the cupboard above the sink.

"It hasn't been weeks. I was just out with the girls." I stopped to think about the last time.

"You see. I'm right. You can't even remember. Here," he said as he handed me a glass of wine. "What have you been doing?"

"Writing a book."

"What?" he asked.

I gestured at all of the little yellow stickers surrounding us. "It's not exactly a book; more like a loose series of articles that might make a book someday."

"Eh, by the way, everyone got your link to that ladies e-zine. We loved your 'Hollywood Ending' story. The title's a little harsh, don't you think?"

"I know, I know."

"Still, *cara,* we're all very proud that you were featured on the front page and everything. *Complimenti*! If you were around more often we could tell you these things in person. If the book is anything like the article you may have something there."

"Thanks."

"Okay now, get dressed. We're going out for dinner and you can tell me all about this book and your plans for it."

I didn't really have any plans for the book, but since I had over 200 pages I thought I should at least finish what I'd started and get a professional opinion. I did a Google search for editors and found one who I liked out in Vancouver. I sent Mel the manuscript in June and forgot about it until August when she sent me her evaluation and her annotated copy.

I stared at her e-mail for a long time, afraid to open the attachments. I rested my forehead on my desk. I was mortified. How could I have sent a complete stranger 200-plus pages of total nonsense? What was I thinking?

The moment of truth finally arrived. A bad evaluation meant that even though I'd tried my best and failed, I could still pat myself on the back and move on. It was, after all, quite an accomplishment. I'd never written anything this substantial in my entire writing career. That was my preferred option, the lazy one. Book—check.

On the other hand, even a marginally good evaluation would mean there was potential there. It also meant rewrites. I would have to invest many more hours. I couldn't abandon it and leave it an orphan. I'd have to finish what I'd started.

I opened the attachments and read the evaluation first. It was thorough and indicated that the manuscript was solid. I read the highly scored sections with equal parts enthusiasm and doubt. I read the evaluation twice to make sure she had actually reviewed *my* manuscript and not someone else's.

It was easy to identify those sections that required work. I'd recognized them instinctively as I wrote them. I had only the bare bones of a structure and a hint of a voice. But it was enough to work with.

The editor's note read, "The first draft is for yourself. The second draft is for your readers."

Readers? Her list was long and I was tired. For a split second I contemplated telling my friends that the evaluation was poor and that I had decided to abandon the project. But leaving this project would be like abandoning a child—the child I had never had. There are so many ways to give birth. Couldn't this be one of them? I could nurture the book along and take pride as it grew into its own. I knew what my mother would say about the book being the clay and me having to nurture it, not to mention 12 years of Catholic school training: finish what you start. I decided to continue.

Mel recommended setting up a blog in parallel with the book so I could hone my voice and establish a reading public I could present to a potential publisher. She mentioned several blogs that had been made into books. "Use these as guides," she said.

"Mel, what am I going to write about? I'm not a celebrity, I hate cooking and I'm not a journalist. I'm in sales. Don't you think it would be better if I had a cool career like fashion designer, lifestyle columnist, motivational speaker or spy? You know, the kind of women they write about in sitcoms or movies?"

"Cat," her voice echoed over Skype, "you've got an exciting life. So many people will live vicariously through your travels and adventures. Use them. You're the interesting best friend, the one who tries everything first and reports back to the girls. You're a real woman, with a real job, and you live in the real world."

"Yeah, well sometimes reality isn't all it's cracked up to be."

"It's your ability to bounce back. If I may quote you," she added, "'as long as I'm alive, I'm never really done.' There are lots of women out there who could benefit from your experience."

Suddenly any residual sadness I felt about Luca was replaced with a newfound serenity and a sense of purpose. When I opened the full manuscript I saw the chapters Mel had tagged "keep for the book" and others that said "better for the blog." In September 2009 I launched my blog, The Café Girl Chronicles, and discovered a new world and a new me.

CHAPTER 26:
ALL THE COLORS IN THE BOX

Any color but beige. —Cat

Finally the clock ticked over on New Year's Eve and I found myself in the double-digit decade of 2010. It was like turning a page, a chance to start over. It was a new me facing a new decade with a new hard-won perspective on life and love. Going forward, things would be different.

When I typed those first tentative lines during those long, lonely afternoons in the Café Audace, little did I know where those thoughts would lead me. At the time I felt I was in the middle of a long, dark tunnel with only a match for illumination. I could never have imagined that one year later I would come out the other side happier and with a new purpose, literally needing to wear sunglasses.

I stared out of the floor-to-ceiling windows and squinted at the sun glittering off the office towers in Mexico City's exclusive Lomas Reforma district. I looked at the color chips and fan decks strewn on the boardroom table. The colors looked washed out. I could barely see my laptop screen from the glare. I'd never be able to give my presentation in this sun-drenched boardroom.

I heard a click followed by a steady hum as motorized solar screens slid down between the double-glazed window panes. The room was pleasantly darker and felt a few degrees cooler. My eyes adjusted to the change in light. Ah, that's more like it.

"*Hola Guerita*. Is better?" Ignacio Sanchez asked from the doorway as he removed his hand from the wall-mounted control panel. *Guerita* is a term of endearment for a light-skinned, light-eyed woman. It literally means "blondie." I was baptized Guerita during one of my many trips to Mexico City and the name stuck. I liked it.

I crossed the room to shake hands with the sales director of one of the largest real estate development firms in Mexico. His Armani suit was cut perfectly to show off his wide shoulders and narrow hips. A white shirt with monogrammed cuffs peeked out from underneath his starched shirt-sleeves. His tie was a riot of color. The formalities finished, he stepped in and kissed me on each cheek and smiled.

"*Perfecta*," I said.

"And so are you. I'm happy to see you smiling again."

Poor Ignacio, I'd seen him the year before, only a few weeks after my return from Italy, and I hadn't been myself. He'd known something was very wrong when I turned down a night of dancing at Antillano, a popular salsa club. The sadness I'd felt was so deep I could no longer experience the joy and lightness in the salsa music. It no longer moved me. I recalled how over dinner that night, Ignacio had given me a piece of advice that I took to heart.

"Guerita, it hurts me to see such sadness in your eyes, and all this over…"—and here he made a dismissive motion with his hand—"a man who isn't worth a second thought, let alone a second glance from such a beautiful woman. Listen to your old friend Ignacio. Don't waste tears or time."

"Am I smiling?" I asked, back in the present.

"Ah, that's the Guerita I know. And now, what are we talking about today?"

"What women want."

"*¡Ay, caramba*! If you can tell us that you have unlocked a secret for the ages."

"In color, in color," I added.

"We're all ears," I heard a chorus of voices say behind me. The design team had arrived. They were a young, well-dressed group of 30-something designers eager to learn the latest in color strategy from their own personal color expert.

I was dressed all in black on purpose. It was my canvas, and as they watched I casually draped a turquoise and indigo crinkle silk scarf around my neck. It intensified my green eyes.

A second scarf of warm reds, deep oranges and golds flowed out of my computer case like lava onto the boardroom table. The colors were the perfect accent for my hair.

A third scarf, a mixture of bright mauves and pinks, lay coiled on the table like whipped icing on a cupcake. Like most of my presentations, this one would be show and tell.

"And so, what do women want, Guerita?" a chubby-faced Manuel asked, his brown eyes shining as he gestured at the color chips strewn about the boardroom table.

"Any color but beige."

"*¡Eso es!*" they all said at once, exchanging high fives.

"Not all colors," I continued, "but the right colors. Unless she's a professional, the average woman is what I call an in-*fear*-ior decorator, with an emphasis on *fear*. F-E-A-R. It's only with a little time, practice and help from you that she gains enough confidence to add some color to her life. Too much color can be intimidating, and not enough can be stifling. Achieving the right mix of colors in a room, a wardrobe or even life is all about balance and selecting from the right palette."

The presentation was over in less than an hour. I thanked the team for its time and attention and began packing up as they filed back to their offices. I heard a knock on the door, turned and saw Ignacio.

"Well done, Guerita, as usual."

"Thank you, Ignacio. They're a great group."

He paused in the doorway. "*Bailar conmigo*?"

"Salsa! Si!"

"Excelente! When do you fly home?"

"Tomorrow morning."

"Then you may as well check out of the hotel tonight and we'll go right from the club to the airport."

I swallowed hard, smiled and nodded. Why not? I thought. Next month I would turn 50. What a great way to end my fourth decade, spent but satisfied from dancing all night.

Once again I arrived back in Montreal in the middle of February. This time I returned to the warmth and comfort of my own apartment. I dropped my bags in the entry way and admired the rising sun as it lit the Serengeti-colored walls of my living room. I was reminded of the plains of

Thandie's beloved country and her words, "Come home to Africa." I knew what she meant every time I returned to my richly painted apartment. I was finally home. My home . . .

I heard salsa music. Wow, I thought. Not only is the place colorful, it comes with its own soundtrack. Then I realized it was my cell phone ringing.

"Cat speaking."

"I thought you could only train dogs to speak."

"Ha, who is this?"

"It's me, Jon. How was the Mexican presentation?"

"Great."

"Where are you?"

"Montreal, why?"

"I've got some good news."

"Yeah?"

"Do you remember how you said you've always wanted to live in Europe?"

"God, you got some memory."

"We just closed a joint venture deal with a European manufacturer. So now we have manufacturing and warehousing, but we need to beef up the local sales efforts. Would you like to move?"

"Where?"

"Anywhere you want. You can still work from home wherever that happens to be. You know, it's that hat thing your grandmother always talked about. London? Brussels? Paris? You tell me."

There was a long pause as I tried to process the implication of his words. Paris.

"Cat? Are you still there?"

A month later. Annie dropped her cigarette in a water-filled yogurt container. She set the container in the corner of my concrete balcony, slid back the patio door and stepped into my living room.

"You realize you're leaving Montreal at the best time of year. Look at this view." She turned me around by the shoulders to face the Lachine Canal, the trees dressed for spring. "Jobs and men come and go but Montreal is a constant."

"You're right, Annie. I'm not above having an occasional affair with London, Paris or Rome, but for all intents and purposes I'm married to

Montreal. I'm just going to try this on for size, see how it fits, experience the local color, go native. The plan is to live in a different city for a few weeks. I'll be home in three months."

Annie glanced at her watch and settled herself on my couch. She fished a compact and some lip gloss out of her purse and refreshed her make-up.

"What do your folks think of all this?"

"What can they say? I've always lived out of a suitcase. It's who I am."

"A little red suitcase." Annie pointed to the three suitcases in the middle of my now fully furnished living room. "And how long have *those* been there?"

"Not long."

"Are you sure there isn't anything else I can help you with?"

"Besides taking me to the airport? And checking on the tenants while I'm gone? Nah, I'm good. Thanks, kiddo, for everything."

"Anytime. Are you ready to go?"

"Yes."

I pulled on the telescoping handle of my large olive-colored Travel Pro suitcase and latched on a smaller matching bag so it formed one portable unit. Annie bent down to pick up the little red suitcase. She tried lifting it with two fingers. It didn't move.

"*Voyons*, it's not empty this time. Cat, what do you have in here ...bricks?"

She grasped the handle firmly and lifted it.

"My book manuscript and all my notes."

"You mean your dreams."

"Yes. My dreams."

ACKNOWLEDGMENTS

This is the most intimidating part of writing this book because there were so many people who were instrumental in nudging, nurturing and nagging it along that I'm afraid I might leave someone out.

I'll start with my grandmother, to whom I've dedicated this book. Thanks to Vincenza Cristine Ricci, who, as a milliner, knew a thing or two about hats, and even more about her granddaughter.

Thanks also to my parents and six siblings, who provided an endless source of stories and entertainment over the years. My mom, Louise, passed on her creativity gene to all her children. My dad, James B., encouraged us to take risks even if it meant looking silly. My brothers Jimmy, Michael and Danny never missed a cue in their supporting roles. My sisters: Margaret Mary prayed this book possible and kept me off the down escalator to hell; Bethie never gave a compliment she didn't mean, and the ones she gave meant a lot; and Donna held my hand through the entire creative process and endless rewrites. For MJK because he asked.

Thanks to the Mulgrews, who are always there when you need them. The Viccarone girls gave me a basic knowledge of Italian and my sense of style. Julie Ricci created a monster when she gave her ten-year-old niece a used Underwood typewriter that launched a career. The O'Malley cousins continue to provide food and shelter to the "Yank" who still shows up at their door.

Thanks to my two best friends, Patty Iasiello and Regina Hauck, who provided a lifetime of material, most of it too embarrassing to print. KP Graham worked every night of her freshman year to keep me at the Academy. Joanne McGonagle gave great advice, support and encouragement for both the book and blog. Thanks also to Anyk "you'll be fine" Desfossés, who, if she didn't exist, I'd have to invent; to Marlene Shoucair, who believed in me every step of the way; to Vivian Doyle-Kelly for always making me laugh even when there was nothing to laugh about; and to Micha Saad, who always asked the same question every time I saw her: "Did you start?" Glad you asked!

Thanks to The Montreal Café Girls: Micha, Eva, Randa, Lina, Lucy, Marina, Linda, Nanou and Ursula—without them I would never have seen the inside of as many cafés as I have throughout the years. To The Vancouver Café Girls for their loyal support. To all the loyal readers of The Café Girl Chronicles who took the time to read the posts and always leave an encouraging word or two.

Denyse and Pierre took good care of my place in absentia and have often allowed me to run away from home to theirs. Riccardo Del Dotto and Helen Samson always provided a soft place to land, food to eat, wine to drink and a lifetime of friendship. Robin and Dale Palin my Canadian "family" and dear friends who supported all of my creative endeavors with love and enthusiasm. Susan Beauchamp always listened and made me laugh no matter how bad things got.

Gratitude to Giacomo Indri, the go-to guy for anything and everything; David Shibatani, friend and author who coached me along with an endless supply of encouragement; Joanne Ivanski for reading and re-reading every version and providing feedback and clear vision throughout the entire process; Julie Wesson, who planted a seed; Michael D. Zinicola and David Bailey, long-time spectators to my love life who gave loving and helpful advice when I couldn't think straight; and Dr. Talaat Guirguis, teacher, psychologist, philosopher, mathematician and friend who held my hand and didn't let go.

Thanks also to Rick Duha who always said yes to my ideas, no matter how far-fetched or far-flung they were. To Serene Pang who unknowingly provided the marketing catalyst for this book through one of her great presentations. To Melva McLean, my editor extraordinaire, whose talent is exceeded only by her patience in this long process. She was the perfect midwife for the book. To Lana Okerlund for her careful proofing and continuity review. To Steven Schultz, friend and long-time collaborator who believed in all of my crazy ideas and dreams; he was always ready, pencil in hand. To Helen Samson, a talented graphic designer, illustrator and friend who sent me right back to the keyboard every time I wanted to quit. And to Jim Sweeney, PR magician and friend, who always had time to listen and gave invaluable advice.

ABOUT THE AUTHOR

Catherine Larose is the author of The Café Girl Chronicles blog, www.cafegirlchronicles.wordpress.com. When she isn't traveling the world for her job as a color marketer, Cat enjoys life in Montreal, Canada. *Any Color but Beige* is her first book, and she is busy working on a second.

BRING OUT THE COLOR IN YOUR LIFE

Any Color but Beige comes with its own set of six professionally selected color palettes all in the form of bookmarks.

Girls' Night Out
Quiet Moments
Adventure Road
Brand New Me
Next
Ah Spa

These bookmarks are **free** to anyone who has purchased the book. Here's how to order.

1. Log on to my website:
www.cafegirlchronicles.wordpress.com
2. Tell me where to send them
3. Please use promo code: A1C5B9B

Limit one set per reader. Offer good while supplies last.

CPSIA information can be obtained at www.ICGtesting.com
Printed in the USA
LVOW071455161111

255293LV00002B/126/P